D1147655

Problem Solving, Reasoning and Numeracy

Pat Beckley, Ashley Compton
Jane Johnston and
Harriet Marland

Supporting Development in
the Early Years Foundation Stage

continuum

Continuum International Publishing Group

The Tower Building	80 Maiden Lane
11 York Road	Suite 704
London, SE1 7NX	New York, NY 10038

www.continuumbooks.com

© Pat Beckley, Ashley Compton, Jane Johnston and Harriet Marland 2010

Photographs 1.1, 1.3, 1.4, 1.5, 2.1 and 2.3 used by kind permission of Paul
Hopkins (MMI educational consultancy services - http://www.mmiweb.org.uk).
Photograph 2.5 used by kind permission of Emma Jordan (E-Services www.
emmajordan-eservices.co.uk).
Photograph 2.2 used by kind permission of Tracy Gannon, Headteacher, Ripley
Infant School.
All other photographs are sourced by the authors.

British Library Cataloguing-in-Publication Data
A catalogue record for this book is available from the British Library.

ISBN: 978-1-4411-8959-2 (hardcover)
      978-1-4411-6474-2 (paperback)

Library of Congress Cataloging-in-Publication Data
Problem solving, reasoning, and numeracy / Pat Beckley ... [et al.].
    p. cm. – (Supporting development in the early years foundation stage
Includes bibliographical references and index.
ISBN: 978-1-4411-8959-2 (hardback)
ISBN: 978-1-4411-6474-2 (paperback.)
 1. Child development. 2. Mathematics – Study and teaching (Elementary)
 3. Learning, Psychology of. I. Beckley, Pat. II. Title. III. Series.

HQ772.P76 2010
305.231–dc22
                                             2010002900

Typeset by Newgen Imaging Systems Pvt Ltd, Chennai, India
Printed and bound in Great Britain by the MPG Books Group

Contents

Author Details

The authors of this book are all experienced educationalists with expertise in early years or mathematics or both.

Pat Beckley

Pat is the Academic Coordinator for the 3–7 age phase on the PGCE Primary course at Bishop Grosseteste University College Lincoln, United Kingdom. She has taught children in the 3–11 age range, becoming the leader in each age phase, including organizing an Early Years Unit for a number of years. As an Advanced Skills Teacher Pat supported colleagues and settings, leading INSET and formulating Action Plans. Her work used research to inform her practice in schools. This included an Advanced Diploma in Special Educational Needs with a focus on early years, an M.Ed. based on approaches to early years literacy and participation in the Effective Early Years Project. Working with the Children's University in Hull, United Kingdom, she helped to coordinate community involvement in children's learning. She is currently completing an Ed. D. thesis which concerns a comparison of approaches to early years literacy between Lincolnshire, England and Hedmark, Norway. Her work has included liaison with educationalists in Norway, attendance at international conferences and participation as an executive member of the national organization TACTYC (Training, Advancement and Co-operation in Teaching Young Children).

Ashley Compton

Ashley Compton is a Senior Lecturer on the BA (Hons) in Primary Education with QTS at Bishop Grosseteste University College Lincoln, United Kingdom. Her interests include music, mathematics and creativity. Chronicling the development of her two young children has stimulated Ashley's fascination with the early years. She has taught in schools in Canada and the United Kingdom and has also worked as a maths advisory teacher for Lincolnshire.

Jane Johnston

Jane, one of the series editors, is a Reader in Education at Bishop Grosseteste University College Lincoln United Kingdom. She has worked as an early years primary classroom practitioner and in early years and primary education initial training. She has a particular interest in early years scientific development (Emergent Science) and is passionate about supporting early years development through exploration and play. Her many publications reflect this interest and she is the author of many books, articles and chapters on early years and science education, including *Early Explorations in Science* (2005), Maidenhead: Open University Press and *Early Childhood Studies* in collaboration with L. Nahmad-Williams (2009), *Early Childhood Studies.* Essex: Pearson Education Limited.

Harriet Marland

Harriet is Head of Department of Professional Development in Education at Bishop Grosseteste University College Lincoln, United Kingdom. She worked in both primary and secondary schools before moving into teacher education. She is fascinated by children's thinking, particularly when this is applied to investigating the number system. She has written on Mathematics for the Mathematical Association contributing to a range of publications focusing on issues such as sharing mathematics with parents, children's use of calculators and the development of mental methods in the teaching of maths.

Series Editors' Preface

Chapter Outline

Introduction to the series

Before the 10 year strategy (DfES, 2004) and the Childcare Act of 2006, provision for children under 5 years of age was encompassed in a variety of guidance, support and legislation; *Curriculum Guidance for the Foundation Stage* (QCA, 2000), the *Birth to Three Matters* framework (Surestart, 2003), and the *National Standards for Under 8s Daycare and Childminding* (DfES, 2003). This was confusing for many professionals working with young children. The introduction of Early Years Foundation Stage (DCSF, 2008), brought together the main features of each and has provided a structure for the provision of care and education for children from birth to 5 years of age. More importantly it recognized the good practice that existed in each sector of provision and gives a framework or support for further development.

Learning in the Early Years Foundation Stage

The four themes that embody the principles of the Early Years Foundation Stage (EYFS), (DCSF, 2008) succinctly embody the important features of early years provision.

A Unique Child, identifies the importance of child centred provision, recognizing the rapid development in young children and that each child is capable of significant achievements during these years. It is important not to underestimate young children, who may be capable of action, thinking beyond our expectations. It is easy to think that children are too young or not experienced enough to engage in some ideas or activities, but we need to be open-minded as children are very good at exceeding our expectations. Some children may have particular talents, whilst others may be 'all-rounders'. Some children may have particular needs or disabilities. Each child is unique and it is our challenge to ensure that we meet their particular needs, supporting them and challenging them in their development.

Positive Relationships are essential whilst we support and challenge children so that they move from dependence to independence, familiarity to unfamiliarity, learning how to be secure and confident individuals who begin to understand themselves and others. Positive relationships are key to all areas of children's development. Emotional development requires children to have attachments and positive relationships, initially with close family members, but increasingly with secondary carers, peers and other adults. The link between emotional and social development is very strong and positive relationships will also help children to become independent and develop new relationships and begin to see their position and role in society. Positive relationships also support language development, understandings about the world, a range of skills and indeed play a part in all development.

The context in which children develop play a vital part in supporting them in all areas of development. These contexts need to be **Enabling Environments**, or environments that are secure and make children feel confident, that stimulate and motivate children and which support and extend their development and learning. The environment is made up of the physical and the atmospheric. Both need to be warm and secure, so that children feel safe and comfortable and both need to be motivating to encourage children to explore and learn. The environmental atmosphere is also created by the social interactions of all concerned, providing the security that enables a child to move away from the familiar and explore the unfamiliar in a secure and safe way. Indoor environments should provide opportunities for social interaction, language development and creative activities. Outdoor environments may encourage children to develop physically and an interest in the world around them and with opportunities to explore the familiar and unfamiliar world.

Learning and Development indicates the importance of individual children's unique development and learning. As every child is unique, so they have different learning and development needs and will develop in different ways and at different rates. It is important not to assume that all children develop at the same rate. We know that some children begin to walk or talk at a very early age, whilst others take longer, but this does not indicate what they are capable of achieving later in life. Provision for all children needs to be differentiated. In the early years, this is best done by open-ended activities and differentiated interaction and support. Open-ended activities allow children to use and develop from previous experiences and to differentiate for themselves. Support through modelling, questioning and direction can come from experienced peers and adults and will enable the individual child to develop at a rate appropriate for them.

Working within the Early Years Foundation Stage is not without it challenges. Whilst the principles recognize the individual nature of children and their needs, providing this is a different matter. The Early Years Foundation Stage encompasses children in two traditionally distinct phases of development; from birth to 3 years of age and from 3 to 5 years of age. It involves the integration of three overlapping, but traditionally distinct areas of care; social, health and education. Children will have different needs at different ages and in different areas and stages within the EYFS and the challenge is for professionals to meet these diverse needs. It maybe that the norm for children at each age and stage is quite wide and that as many children fall outside of the norm as within it. Care is needed by professionals to ensure that they do not assume that each child is 'normal'.

In order to effectively support children's development in the Early Years Foundation Stage professionals need to have an understanding of child development and share knowledge and understanding in their area of expertise with others whose expertise may lie elsewhere. Professionals from different areas of children's care and provision should work together and learn from each other. Social care, health, educational professionals can all learn from an integrated approach and provide more effective provision as a result. Even within one discipline, professionals can support each other to provide more effective support. Teachers, teaching assistants, special needs coordinators and speech therapists who work in an integrated way can provide better support for individuals. Paediatricians, paediatric nurses, physiotherapist, opticians etc., can support the health care and physical development of children in a holistic way. Early years professionals, behaviour therapists and child psychologists can support the social and emotional development of children. This notion of partnership or teamwork is an important part of integrated working, so that the different types of professionals who work with young children value and respect each other, share knowledge and understanding and always consider the reason for integration; the individual child, who should be at the heart of all we do. Good integrated working does not value one aspect of development above all others or one age of children more than another. It involves different professionals, from early career to those in leadership roles, balancing the different areas of development (health, social, emotional and educational) and ages, ensuring that the key principles of good early years practice are maintained and developed through appropriate interpretation and implementation of the Early Years Foundation Stage.

Another challenge in the Early Years Foundation Stage is to consider the child's holistic progression from birth, through the EYFS to Key Stage 1 and beyond. Working with children in the Early Years Foundation Stage is like being asked to write the next chapter of a book; in order to do this effectively, you need to read the earlier chapters of the book, get to know the main characters and the peripheral characters, understand the plot and where the story is going. However, all the time you are writing you need to be aware that you will not complete the book and that someone else will write the next chapter. If professionals know about individual children, their families, home lives, health and social needs, they will understand problems, issues, developmental needs and be better placed to support the child. If they know where are child will go next, about the differences between the provision in the EYFS and KS1 and even KS2 (remembering the international definition of early childhood is birth to 8 years of age), they can help the child to overcome the difficulties of transition. Transitions occur in all areas of life and at all ages. When we start new jobs, move house, get married, meet new people, go to university, the transition takes some adjustment and involves considerable social and emotional turmoil, even when things go smoothly. As adults we enter these transitions with some knowledge and with a degree of choice, but young children are not as knowledgeable about the transitions that they experience and have less choice in the decisions made about transitions. Babies will not understand that their mother will return soon, small children will not understand that the friends that they made at playgroup are not attending the same nursery or that the routines they have been used to at home and at playgroup have all changed now that they have gone to nursery or started in the foundation unit at school. Professionals working with children, as they move though the many transitions they experience in the first 5 years, need to smooth the pathway for children to ensure that they have smooth and not difficult transitions.

An example of holistic thematic play

Whilst sitting outside a café by the sea in the north of England, the following play was observed. It involved four children representing the whole of early years from about 2 years of age to about 8 years of age; one was about 2 years of age, another about 3 years of age, one about 5 years of age and the fourth about 7 or 8 years of age. The two older children climbed on top of a large wooden seal sculpture and started to imagine that they were riding on top of a swimming seal in the sea. They were soon joined by the 3-year-old child who sat at the foot of the sculpture. 'Don't sit there' said the eldest, 'You are in the sea, you will drown. Climb on the tail, out of the sea'. The two older children helped the 3 year old to climb onto the tail and she and the 5 year old started to slide down the tail and climb up again. Then the children began to imagine that the cars parked nearby were 'whales' and the dogs out with their owners were 'sharks' and as they slid down the tail they squealed that they should 'mind the sharks, they will eat you'. The 5 year old asked what the people sitting outside the café were and the 8 year old said 'I think they can be fishes swimming in the sea'. 'What about the chairs and tables?' asked the 3 year old, to which the older children replied that, 'they can be fishes too'.

At this point, the 2 year old came up to the children and tried to climb up the seal. The three children welcomed her, helped her climb up onto the tail and join them and asked her what her name was. They continued to play and then the mother of the eldest child came to see if the 2 year old was ok and not being squashed in the sliding down the tail. The children did not welcome the interference of an adult and asked her to go away, because 'we are playing, we are playing'. The mother helped the 2 year old to climb down off the seal and the child started to 'swim' on the floor back towards the seal and the other children. The mother said, 'Oh you are getting dirty, get up', but the child kept on 'swimming'. 'Are you being a dog' said the mother 'don't crawl', but the child shook her head and carried on 'swimming' towards the seal, avoiding the fish and sharks!

In this play episode, the children were engaged in holistic play involving aspects of

- Personal, Social and Emotional Development (cooperation);
- Language, Literacy and Communication (communicating with each other and with adults);
- Knowledge and Understanding of the World (applying ideas about animals that live in the sea);
- Creative Development (imaginative play, involving both ludic or fantasy play and epistemic play, or play involving their knowledge).

The adult intervention was, in this case, unhelpful and did not aid the play and illustrates the importance of adults standing back and watching before they interact or intervene.

Supporting development in the Early Years Foundation Stage

This book series consists of six books, one focusing on each of the key areas of the Early Years Foundation Stage and with each book having a chapter for each of the strands that make up that key area of learning. The chapter authors have between them a wealth of expertise in early years provision, as practitioners, educators, policy-makers and authors and are thus well placed to give a comprehensive overview of the sector.

The series aims to look at each of the key areas of the EYFS and support professionals in meeting challenges of implementation and effectively supporting children in their early development. The aim is to do this by helping readers, whether they are trainee, early career or lead professionals:

- to develop deeper understanding of the Early Years Foundation Stage,
- to develop pedagogical skills and professional reflectiveness,
- to develop their personal and professional practice.

Although the series uses the sub-divisions of the key areas of learning and strands within each key area, the authors strongly believe that all areas of learning and development are equally important and inter-connected and that development and learning for children in the early years and beyond is more effective when it is holistic and cross curricular. Throughout the series, links are made between one key area and another and in the introduction to each book specific cross curricular themes and issues are explored. We recognize that language development is a key element in social and emotional development, as well as development in mathematics and knowledge and understanding of the world. We also recognize that the development of attitudes such as curiosity and social skills are key to development in all areas, recognizing the part that motivation and social construction play in learning. In addition, the books use the concept of creativity in its widest sense in all key areas of development and learning and promote play as a key way in which children learn.

Although we believe it is essential that children's learning be viewed holistically, there is also a need for professionals to have a good knowledge of each area of learning and a clear understanding of the development of concepts within each area. It is hoped that each book will provide the professional with appropriate knowledge about the learning area which will then support teaching and learning. For example, if professionals have an understanding of children's developing understanding of cardinal numbers, ordinal numbers, subitizing and numerosity in problem solving, reasoning and numeracy then they will be better equipped to support children's learning with developmentally appropriate activities. Although many professionals have a good understanding of high quality early years practice, their knowledge of specific areas of learning may vary. We all have areas of the curriculum that we particularly enjoy or feel confident in and equally there are areas where we feel we need more support and guidance. This is why each book has been written by specialists in each area of learning, to provide the reader with appropriate knowledge about the subject area itself and suggestions for activities that will support and promote children's learning.

Within each chapter, there is an introduction to the key area, with consideration of the development of children in that key area from birth to 3 years of age; 3 to 5 years of age; into Key Stage 1 (5 to 7 years of age). In this way we consider the holistic development of children, the impact of that development on the key area and the transition from one stage of learning to another in a progressive and 'bottom-up' way. Chapters also contain research evidence and discussions of and reflections on the implications of that research on practice and provision. Boxed features in each chapter contain practical examples of good practice in the key area, together with discussions and reflective tasks for early career professionals and early years leaders/managers, which are designed to help professionals at different stages in their career to continue to develop their professional expertise.

Jane Johnston and Lindy Nahmad-Williams

Books in the series

Broadhead, P., Johnston, J., Tobbell, C. & Woolley, R. (2010) *Personal, Social and Emotional Development.* London: Continuum

Callander, N. & Nahmad-Williams, L. (2010) *Communication, Language and Literacy.* London: Continuum

Beckley, P., Compton, A., Johnston, J. & Marland, H. (2010) *Problem Solving, Reasoning and Numeracy.* London: Continuum

Cooper, L., Johnston, J., Rotchell, E. & Woolley, R. (2010) *Knowledge and Understanding of the World.* London: Continuum

Cooper, L. & Doherty, J., (2010) *Physical Development.* London: Continuum

Compton, A., Johnston, J., Nahmad-Williams, L. & Taylor, K. (2010) *Creative Development.* London: Continuum

References

DCSF (2008) *The Early Years Foundation Stage; Setting the Standard for Learning, Development and Care for Children from Birth to Five; Practice Guidance.* London: DCSF

DfES (2003) *National Standards for Under 8s Daycare and Childminding.* London: DfES

DfES (2004) *Choice for Parents, the Best Start for Children: A Ten Year Strategy for Children.* London: DfES

QCA (2000) *Curriculum Guidance for the Foundation Stage.* London: DFEE

Surestart, (2003) *Birth to Three Matters.* London: DfES

Introduction to Problem Solving, Reasoning and Numeracy

Chapter Outline

Problem solving, reasoning and numeracy

Mathematical development in the early years is recognized as important to lay the foundations for later development (Williams, 2008). Mathematical development in all areas, that is, understanding of number, calculating, shape, measures etc. occurs in a holistic way and so in this introduction we will focus on this holistic development.

Problem-solving involves children in making decisions for themselves and as discussed in the series book on Creative Development (Compton et. al., 2010) problem solving is a creative enterprise (de Bono, 1992), enabling children to take risks, make decisions for themselves and develop thinking skills. Problem solving is also an element in personal and social development (see Broadhead et. al., 2010), physical development (Cooper and Doherty, 2010) and scientific and technological development (see Cooper et. al., 2010). In many cases, especially in scientific and technological development mathematical problem solving is involved. For example, children using wooden blocks to make a tall structure will consider the shape and strength of the individual blocks and the structure as a whole. They can count the number of blocks used, measure how high the resulting structure is and in the process develop both fine and gross motor skills. They will be able to try out different designs and see which structure is the most stable, the tallest or the uses the most blocks.

Reasoning has links to Toulmin's (1958) theory of argumentation and is a skill that we often do not associate with young children. Providing a strong argument is part of language development (see Callander and Nahmad-Williams, 2010), knowledge and understanding of the world (see Cooper et. al., 2010), and social development (see Broadhead et. al., 2010). While reasoning, children need to provide reasons for claims and evidence that support these claims. They also need to develop persuasive language and the ability to counter-argue. Young children are more likely to use deductive reasoning, where they use the evidence from their experience, rather than inductive reasoning, where they make inferences about unobserved events based on previous observation or experiences. However, the way children think is not always logical to an adult. Young children when asked to sort and tidy a cupboard in the classroom containing a range of objects such as rolls of sellotape, balls, skipping ropes, scissors, crayons and other stationary items and play equipment made the following decisions based on reasoning:

- Rolls of sellotape and balls went together because as one child reasoned they were both 'round', while another child put them together so that the sellotape could be used to mend punctures in the balls.
- Scissors, crayons and sellotape went together because all were used while drawing, cutting and sticking.
- Sellotape and crayons were put together because the sellotape could be used to stick broken crayons back together.
- Items were ordered according to size with small items on the top shelf and big items on the bottom.
- Items were counted and put in order of number.

In this way, everyday activities involve reasoning and numeracy. Numeracy is involved in all aspects of children's development. Children develop the language of numeracy, linking numbers to words, identifying size, shape, amount, distance etc. (see Callander and Nahmad-Williams, 2010) and use these words in investigations into time, place and scientific phenomena (see

Cooper et. al., 2010), where they may also use mathematical reasoning and simple calculations.

Young children are likely to develop problem solving, reasoning and numeracy skills when introduced a wide range of open-ended activities that encourage them to think for themselves. They can be encouraged to solve problems and develop understanding of cause and effect. They can be challenged to test out ideas, solve simple problems set by adults or decided by themselves and discuss their ideas comparing them with the ideas of others and encouraging them to make causal links. This may not mean that the reasoning is accurate, but it should be based on evidence or reasoning. For example, children may assume that big animals are older than small ones, or big objects heavier than small ones. They may reason that a small fat container contains more than a tall thin one.

Holistic development in problem solving, reasoning and numeracy

In looking at children's holistic development in problem solving, reasoning and numeracy, we will look at Piaget's (1950) stages of development. These theories are still a good basis for beginning to understand children's development, although they have been subject to criticism because of the small sample used in his initial study, the assertive nature of his theories and rigidity of stages and the ages assigned to them (Bruner, et. al., 1956). Piaget's theories have also formed the basis for much further research and developed understanding of the way in which children learn.

In the earliest stage of development, the sensori-motor stage (Piaget, 1950), children assimilate information through their senses and via experiences. They learn about the mathematical world by extending and modifying ideas and building up mental pictures of the world. At the pre-operational stage, children are making progress and developing, but their ideas are not always logical. They may believe that a tall thin cup has more drink in it that a short fat one, or that you have added to a playdough ball when you change its shape from a sausage to a ball. At the symbolic stage, children will begin to increasingly recognize symbols, such as words or number signs, which have meaning to them and so language becomes important in mental imagery and understanding about the mathematical world. In the intuitive stage of development, the child's perceptions continue to be important to their thinking and a lack of reversibility is characteristic. They continue to believe that changes in objects equate to changes in quantity or number and they are unable to think about several features of an object at once (conservation), or sort using a number of criteria at the same time or handle variables in mathematical investigation. I have deliberately avoided assigning ages to each of these stages as we now believe that children are capable of quite advanced thinking at an early age. Indeed, there has been evidence in many areas that children are able to operate concretely and abstractly at earlier ages than we had considered possible; Piaget's (1950) last stages concern the ability for concrete and abstract thought (see below). In the concrete operational stage, children's thinking gradually becomes more co-ordinated, rational and adult-like and they can think logically if they can manipulate the object that they are thinking about. So children can change the shape of their playdough ball/sausage and will be able to understand that the mass has remained the same and not been added to or detracted from. In the formal operation stage, thought by Piaget (1950) to be relevant only for much older children and adults, children begin to rely more on ideas than the need to manipulate objects and their thinking becomes more abstract. They are able to solve mental problems and to build up mental models of the world. There is evidence that many young children can solve abstract problems, although not consistently.

Recent interest in cognitive acceleration (the process of supporting the construction of children's ideas) has focused on children's cognitive abilities being accelerated by brain stimulation. However there is little real research evidence to say that the programmes that purport to accelerate cognition have any effect. Research into cognitive acceleration carried out at Kings College, London (see Shayer and Adey, 2002) has led to curriculum materials being developed in mathematics and other cognitive areas, which are designed to support cognitive development and accelerate children's thinking skills. The resources are based on Piaget's cognitive theories and stimulate the development of thinking abilities through three pillars of cognitive acceleration:

- cognitive conflict – the conflict children feel when their ideas are different from the ideas held by others and don't fit the evidence of their experiences,
- social construction – when children work cooperatively with others and together construct knowledge by exploring and investigating ideas,
- metacognition – when children understand their own thinking processes so that they can work individually or socially to support their own development.

Examples of holistic cross-curricular activities

Fast food diner

A Foundation Stage unit set up a role-play area at a fast food diner. The children helped the adult professionals to set up the diner, setting up the 'kitchen' (using a toy oven, pots, pans plates etc.), 'serving hatch' (using a shop front), tables and chairs, etc. In the kitchen area, each pot, pan, plate etc. was placed on a silhouette shape to indicate where it should be returned after play to help keep the 'kitchen' tidy and to support shape recognition. In the 'dining area', the children decided that there should be seating for six people, in groups of two and worked out, and collected together, the correct number of condiments (salt and pepper pots, sauce bottles and sugar bowls). They decided what the menu should be: burgers, hotdogs, chips, ice cream, cakes, muffins, soft drinks, tea and coffee. They wrote the menu and decided how much each item should be. In the kitchen, they used playdough to make bread buns, sausages and burgers, adding colour and baking them so they could use in their play. Unbaked play dough became ice cream that could be dispensed into paper cones with a scoop. Lolly sticks were used as chips. A large toy cake broken into ten segments and toy muffins were augmented with cake cases filled with play dough and baked. Paper cups in three different sizes were given by a local fast food store, as were paper hats and aprons. Nesting cardboard boxes (where two small boxes fitted into a larger one and two of these boxes in turn, fitted into an even bigger box) were used as containers for the 'fast food' and paper plates used for 'in-house' dining. Post-its were used to write the orders on and stuck to the side of the 'serving hatch' for the kitchen staff. Waiting staff had to fold paper serviettes into triangular shapes and the place-mats were also different shapes (rectangular, square, triangular and circular) and could be folded to make different shapes.

Six children were playing in the fast food diner and the following exchanges were noted:

> Peter (in apron and hat and with a notepad and pen) *'Hello. what do you want?'*
> Zoe with Josh (as customers) *'Two burgers and coke please'*,
> Josh *'and chips, and chips'*
> Zoe and Josh sit down and wait for their food and Peter shouts in a loud voice to Sunita in the kitchen *'Two burgers and chips and coke'*.
> Zoe says to Josh *'We need to wash our hands.'* Josh asks Peter where he can wash his hands and Peter points to the children's cloakroom on the other side of the classroom. Zoe says, *'You go first and I'll keep the seats.'*

> Sunita passes 2 plates with burgers and chips to Peter who takes them across to Zoe sitting at the table and she asks *'What about the coke?'*, and Peter goes over to the 'serving hatch' and shouts again at Sunita for the cokes, which she brings to the hatch. She has one large cup and one small cup and the children talk about how much coke they have in each cup, *'This one is twice as big as that one.'*

The children are then joined by Zane and Eddie who enter the role-play area and say they want to have a birthday party in the diner. Sunita and Peter want to join the party and so the six children renegotiate their roles, so that Zoe becomes the waitress and cook and the other five children join the party. Zoe brings the large cake over to the table and the children work out that they can share it equally between the five of them, with each child having two slices.

> Zane says it is his birthday and he is 4 years old, *'I was 3 but now I am 4. When it is my next birthday I will be 5 and go to big school. I will be as big as my brother.'*
> *'Do you want ice cream?'* says Zoe, to which all five children say *'Yes'*.
> *'One scoop or two?'* says Zoe. Peter and Sunita want two but the others want one scoop. Zoe starts to look puzzled and goes to and asks the professional *'How many scoops shall I do?* The professional comes into the role play area and starts to help the children to decide how many cones they need and how many scoops altogether.

In this way the children were developing understanding and skills in problem solving, reasoning and numeracy by counting the number of chairs, meals, drinks etc., calculating the total number of orders, drinks, meals etc. They were comparing numbers and shapes, matching the shapes of pots and pans to their silhouette and fitting together boxes in a 3-D tessellation exercise. They were making shapes by folding the serviettes, measuring the amounts of chips and volume of drinks, using non-standard measures. In addition to the mathematical development, the children were exploring in other key areas of the Early Years Foundation Stage (DCSF, 2008):

- personal, social and emotional development – by negotiating, imitating social contexts and interactions, considering health and hygiene and developing relationships (see Broadhead et. al., 2010);
- communication, language and literacy – by reading and writing menus and orders and communicating with each other (see Callander and Nahmad-Williams, 2010);

- knowledge and understanding of the world – by making and designing food and menus (see Cooper et. al., 2010);
- physical development – through fine motor skills in folding paper serviettes (see Cooper and Doherty, 2010);
- creative development – by using their imagination in their role-play, building on their previous knowledge and using it in imaginative contexts (see Compton et. al., 2010).

Shoe shop

In a nursery school for 2-to 5-year-olds, a shoe shop was set up. The shoe shop contained a large collection of different types of footwear: baby bootees, children's shoes of different shapes and sizes, boots, slippers, high-heeled shoes etc. There was a large collection of shoe boxes of different sizes obtained from a local shoe shop and some flat packed boxes of different sizes. A bench and a foot stall were put into the shop for 'customers' to try on their shoes and a long plastic swivel mirror was put there for 'customers' to see their new shoes in. A toy till with plastic round coins was placed by the hatch for 'customers' to pay for their food and the children decided also to make paper money and cut rectangular pieces of paper and made marks on them to indicate different values of money. Smaller rectangular pieces of card became 'credit cards' and small scraps of waste paper became receipts.

In one learning experience, an adult professional enters the shop, as a customer, pushing a pushchair with a doll and asks for a pair of party shoes for her and some slippers for her child. Katy, who is in role as a sales assistant, says that she will have a look for some party shoes, while Ben goes to find some slippers. Katy brings out three pairs of shoes of different sizes. 'Will these all fit me?' said the professional, to which Katy responded by saying 'I think the big ones will, try them on.' Jonnie and Holly enter the shoe shop and Holly says 'They are all big shoes,' and the professional asks, 'What are they bigger than?' Holly identifies that they are bigger than her shoes and the professional asks the children to identify which shoes are big, bigger and biggest. She tries on the biggest shoes and then asks the children how many shoes there are in the pair on her feet. 'Two', says Jonnie and Katy says, 'There are two here as well.' Ben, who has returned with some slippers for the 'baby' says 'I have two slippers.' The professional then asks the children to count the shoes in twos, pointing at the three pairs of shoes and the pair of slippers as the children count, '2, 4, 6, 8'. The professional says, 'So, we have how many pairs of shoes?' to which Katy replies 'Four, four!'. The professional continues 'And we have how many shoes altogether?' and the children all answer '8'.

Ben turns to the 'baby' and tries to put the slippers on. 'They are too big' he says. 'And these shoes are too small for you,' says Katy turning to the professional and pointing to the shoes she has brought to try on. Holly says, 'My feet are getting bigger all the time – my mum says I will grow into my sister's shoes soon.' The children then compare their shoes for size and Holly points out that if they look on the bottom of their shoes they will have numbers on them to say how big they are. They decide to take off their shoes and lay them out in pairs with the smallest at one end of the line and the biggest at the other end of the line. They also count the shoes in ones and twos.

Later, the professional decides to buy one pair of shoes and a pair of slippers, asking 'If I buy these and these how many shoes will I have?' and Katy responds telling her she will have four shoes. The professional then asks Katy how much money she owes and Katy says 'Ten pounds please.' The professional gets the children to help her count out ten plastic £1 coins and gives them to Katy and asks for the shoes to be put into a box. Ben offers to do this and gets a box. 'This box is too small' he says and Holly says, 'Have you got a bigger one? Look, this is bigger,' pointing to a bigger box in the corner.

As the professional goes to leave the shop, she suggests to the children that they might wish to sort the shoes, which are all mixed up. 'Let's put them in order of size' says Jonnie, and the four children sort the shoes and call to the professional to look. She congratulates the children on the sorting and asks them if they could have sorted the toys in any other ways. After some discussion, the children decide that the shoes could be sorted according to colour, type (high-heels, boots, slipper), boy's or girl's, although they do not do this on this occasion.

In this way the children were developing understandings and skills in problem solving, reasoning and numeracy by counting the customers and boxes, counting the shoes in twos, calculating the total number shoes sold and the money collected. They measured feet and shoes. They compared and sorted the shoes according to size, shape numbers and type. In addition to the mathematical development, the children were exploring in other key areas of the Early Years Foundation Stage (DCSF, 2008):

- personal, social and emotional development – by taking on roles and applying the social rules involved with buying and selling, imitating and interacting with each other and the professional in their play (see Broadhead et al., 2010);

- communication, language and literacy – by communicating with each other and defining the roles they were in (see Callander and Nahmad-Williams, 2010);
- knowledge and understanding of the world – in recognizing similarities and differences between themselves and others and that children grow into adults (see Cooper et. al., 2010);
- creative development – by using their imagination in their role play, building on their previous knowledge and using it in imaginative contexts (see Compton et. al., 2010).

The quality of these informal play-based learning experiences as advocated by the Cambridge Primary Review (Alexander, 2009) is far greater than the more formal experiences advocated by the ill-informed, those not involved in education and those policy makers who think they know more than experienced professionals. All of these developments are dependent on the social interactions between the children and the professionals. Adults support the mathematical development by encouraging children, in the first example, to calculate the number of chairs needed or the total number of scoops of ice cream, see patterns in the numbers of scoops, sizes of cups and to solve simple mathematical problems. In the second example, the adult professional was integral to the whole play and, while in role, she encouraged the children to count the shoes in ones and twos, compare the shoes, sort the shoes, calculate the cost of shoes etc. In both examples, language and communication play an important part in the development of skills and understandings in problem solving, reasoning and numeracy. Child-led play activities alone will not help children in this development, but child-led or initiated play activities that include adult interaction can be very supportive of children's mathematic development. This adult interaction should include questioning that is relevant, spontaneous and encouraging of deeper thinking and make use of the rich experiences in the play. Less successful approaches are rigidly planned and executed, often by less mathematically confident teachers, so that children's understanding is not extended through interaction and questioning.

There are many similar activities that will develop children in holistic ways and cover more than one area of development. This support is not always thought (Thompson, 2008) to be present in the Primary Framework for Literacy and Mathematics (DfES, 2006); it is unhelpful and limits the development of young children. Hughes et al. (2000) identify a number of practical and relevant activities to support children's ability to apply mathematical ideas, which are not dissimilar to those appropriate to younger children, such as money taken and spent at a car boot sale and a teddy drive (like a beetle drive but with a teddy bear instead). The primary Project Box (McClure, 2007) set mathematical problems in cross-curricular themes starting from the child's world (Our Classroom and Our School and Inside Outside) to the wider world (Our Wider World, Our Changing World and Our Future World). These involve making tallies and calculating distances on a walk in the unit on Inside Outside to exploring capacity to consider how to save water in the unit on Our Changing World.

As well as role-play and teacher-directed activities, children can develop skills and knowledge in mathematics and other areas through games and rhymes. For example, the game of Jenga involves skills of mental calculation and problem solving together with physical development by supporting the development of fine motor coordination skills (see Cooper and Doherty, 2010). In the game, wooden blocks are placed on top of each other in a tall tower and each player has to remove a block in turn without the tower collapsing and so they have to calculate which block can be removed safely. For very young children light plastic or foam blocks can be used to build a large tower which is as tall and stable as possible, thus involving them in calculating how to make a stable tower. Heads and Tails games can be created by laminating pictures and cutting in half. On one half a number can be written (e.g.3) or a shape coloured in using a whiteboard pen and on the other a calculation to make the number (e.g. 2 + 1 or 4−1) or a matching shape. Children have to turn over a head and tail and can have the whole picture if they recognize that they match. Fishing games can be adapted to include calculations or comparisons which get more complex as the children progress. For example, children will 'catch' a fish with 4 + 2 or 6−2 on and have to complete the calculation in order to keep the fish. Wrong calculations mean the fish has to be thrown back in the pond. The fish can have 2-D or 3-D shapes which the children need to recognize and name to keep the fish or identify how many sides or corners the shape has. A skittle game can be created using plastic bottles and a soft ball (see Ensing and Spencer, 2003) so that children can calculate how many they have knocked over and how many are left as well as calculating a running total. The game can be made more difficult by sticking numbers on the 'skittles' and for children to calculate how many they have by adding the numbers on the felled skittles.

Structure of this book

In the first chapter of this book, Numbers for Labels and for Counting, Ashley Compton provides us with a good insight into the early development of number, helping us to understand the mind of the small child and critiques Piaget's (1950) theories about children's mathematical abilities. She considers the skills associated with number and counting, such as subitizing, numerosity and counting as well as mathematical understandings, such as cardinality and mathematical mark-making. She emphasizes the importance of practical experiences, such as handing and touching objects while counting and provides some useful examples of play activities, such a café, links with language development through use of Kipper's Toy Box (Inkpen, 2008). In Chapter 2, Calculating, Harriet Marland and Jane Johnston identify the key aspects of calculating at different ages in the early years and identify experiences and pedagogical approaches that support calculation. Like Chapter 1 Numbers for Labels and for Counting, Chapter 2, Calculating, advocates play-based practical experiences and this is a common theme in the final chapter, Shape, Space and Measures written by Pat Beckley. In Chapter 2, Calculating, opportunities for calculation are identified in the role-play area, using collections of natural objects and through games. All three chapters identify opportunities for exploring aspects of problem solving, reasoning and numeracy in the child's world and through the child's experiences. In Chapter 3, Shape, Space and Measures, opportunities are identified in the play park, at the fair, as part of construction play and as part of stories such as Little Red Riding Hood. Adult teamwork and liaison are also emphasized in Chapter 3, with discussions on professional teamwork and parents as partners. Indeed, throughout the book, there is a plethora of ideas for professionals working with young children to help develop their problem solving, reasoning and numerical abilities.

The case studies and reflective tasks will also help professionals to reflect on their own practice, consider the theories and research underpinning effective practice and enable them to identify how they can (and why they should) develop their practice. These case studies are designed at two levels: the early career professional and the early years leader. The early years professional may be a student/trainee who is developing their expertise in working with young children and, for them, the reflective tasks encourage them to look at the case studies and engage in some critical thinking on issues that are pertinent for early years education. They will also be able to use the chapters to develop their understanding of issues in problem solving, reasoning and numeracy and try out some of the ideas to develop their skills supporting children in this important area of development. The reflective tasks for early career professionals are also relevant not only to professionals who are in the early part of their career and to help them in their day to day interactions with children, but also to help them to engage in the national debates about good practice and educational theories. The second level of reflective tasks are geared towards the early years leader, who has a strategic role to develop the practice of those who work with them but also the children in the early years setting. They would be interested on the impact on both the adult professional development but raising standards in problem solving, reasoning and numeracy in young children in their setting. The reflective tasks may well be ones that can be addressed as part of a staff meeting or staff development session and can follow the practical tasks so that professionals at all levels can share ideas and experiences, identify factors affecting their support for children, both positive factors and challenges to overcome. In this way professionals can discuss their own and other's practice, share successes, support each other and come to realize that there is not one model of good practice, one recipe, that if we all follow will automatically lead to success in children's development and help the setting achieve outstanding recognition in inspections.

Summary

The main issues identified in this book are

- Problem solving, reasoning and numeracy is an important aspect of children's development in the early years.
- Children's mathematical development requires practical experiences in order to develop both mathematical skills and understandings.
- Mathematical development can be developed effectively through role play, story, rhyme and games.
- Social interaction is very important in supporting mathematical development.
- In particular the development of language and communication is integral to mathematical development.
- There are no specific recipes for success in developing skills and understandings in problem solving, reasoning and numeracy; it is more important to discuss

and share practices, reflections and successes and discuss issues, theories and challenges.

We hope that professionals reading this book both enjoy and find the content useful in their professional lives.

References

Alexander, R. (ed.) (2009), *Children, Their World, Their Education: Final Report and Recommendations of the Cambridge Review*. London: Routledge

Broadhead, P., Johnston, J., Tobbell, C. and Woolley, R. (2010), *Personal, Social and Emotional Development*. London: Continuum

Bruner, J. S., Goodnow, J. J. and Austin, G. A. (1956), *A Study of Thinking*. New York: Wiley

Callander, N and Nahmad-Williams, L. (2010), *Communication, Language and Literacy*. London: Continuum

Compton, A., Johnston, J., Nahmad-Williams, L and Taylor, K. (2010), *Creative Development*. London: Continuum

Cooper, L. and Doherty, J., (2010), *Physical Development*. London: Continuum

Cooper, L., Johnston, J., Rotchell, E. and Woolley, R. (2010), *Knowledge and Understanding of the World*. London: Continuum

DCSF (2008), 'The Early Years Foundation Stage; Setting the Standard for Learning, Development and Care for Children from Birth to Five; Practice Guidance'. London: DCSF

De Bono (1992), *Serious Creativity*. London: Harper Collins

Ensing, J. and Spencer, B. (2003), *Children Learning: Mathematical Development: A Handbook to Support Good Practice for the Early Years*. Walton on Thames: Spencer Publications

Hughes, M., Desforges, C and Mitchell, C. and Carré, C. (2000), *Numeracy and Beyond: Applying Mathematics in the Primary School*. Buckingham: Open University Press

Inkpen, M. (2008), *Kipper's Toybox*. London: Hodder Children's Books

McClure, L. (ed.) (2007), *The Primary Project Box. KS1*. Sheffield: The Curriculum Partnership/GA

Piaget, J. (1950), *The Psychology of Intelligence*. London: Routledge and Kegan Paul.

QCA (2000) *Curriculum Guidance for the Foundation Stage*. London: DFEE

Shayer, M. and Adey, P (eds) (2002), *Learning Intelligence. Cognitive Acceleration Across the Curriculum from 5 to 15 Years*. Buckingham: Open University Press

Surestart, (2003), *Birth to Three Matters. A Framework to Support Children in Their Earliest Years*. London: DfES

Thompson, I. (2008), 'Early Years Foundation Stage: How much does it count?' *Mathematics Teaching*, 210, (September), 40–41

Toulmin, S. (1958), *The Uses of Argument. Cambridge: Cambridge University Press*

Williams, P. (2008), *Independent Review of Mathematics Teaching in Early Years Settings and Primary Schools*. London: DCSF

Numbers as Labels and for Counting

Introduction

Young children live in a world full of numbers. One of the first questions people ask about a newborn baby is how much does she/he weigh. In children's birth notes there are the date and time of birth, the length, weight and head circumference, the birth order, whether single or multiple, the home address and a unique identification number. This collection includes the different sorts of number that people encounter throughout their lives – cardinal, ordinal, nominal and measurements.

Types of numbers

Cardinal numbers are the ones we use for counting, while cardinality involves knowing that the final number of the count represents the total of the objects in the set. When we count one, two, three, four dolls we are using cardinal numbers. If we can answer the question, 'How many?' by saying there are four dolls then we understand cardinality. Ordinal numbers demonstrate the order in which something occurs or the rank something has. We talk about coming second in a race or winning first prize in a raffle. Nominal numbers are the 'labels' in the title 'Numbers as Labels and for Counting'. This is when we use numbers to identify something, such as street address, bus number or National Insurance number. Measures are different from the counting numbers because they are part of continuous scales and the precision depends on the accuracy of the measuring instrument. Measurement will be discussed in the Chapter 3. It is the first three types, cardinal, ordinal and nominal that form the focus of this chapter.

The development of number

Number is an abstract concept, created by humans, rather than a fundamental property of objects. Nevertheless, studies with babies and animals (Antell and Keating, 1983; Boysen 1993; Hauser, 2000; Koechlin et al., 1997; Matsuzawa, 1985; Pepperberg, 1987; Strauss and Curtis, 1981; Wynn, 1996) have demonstrated that some understanding of number is innate, namely subitizing and numerosity.

Subitizing

Subitizing is the ability to recognize the number of objects immediately, without counting them. Close your eyes and try to picture three coins. You were probably able to do this easily and were confident that there were exactly three coins without having to say one, two, three to yourself. That is an example of subitizing. Now try to picture 17 coins. This is not so easy. You might have been totally unable to picture that many or perhaps you imagined a pile of coins that might have had 17 or maybe you were determined so counted them out in your head. The reason that this was more difficult is that subitizing relates only to small numbers: particularly one, two and three. Some young children are able to subitize four as well. As adults you are probably able to visualize some larger numbers as well. If you imagine a pair of dice, it is likely that you can picture dice totals up to 12 by visualizing the spot patterns.

However, it is not clear whether this is using the same brain functions as the subitizing mechanism.

Dehaene (1998) links the ability to subitize the numbers one, two and three with the ways that various cultures around the world have written numbers. In Chinese, Ancient Indian, Roman and Cuneiform notation the numbers one, two and three are made using the appropriate number of sticks but the remaining numbers use different symbols. Both the Mayan and Etruscan notations used repeated symbols for one, two, three and four, before changing to a new symbol. Reading a counting down story with my 2-year-old-daughter, Pippa was able to say immediately when there were three, two or one tadpoles but needed to count, often inaccurately, for larger numbers. The studies mentioned above have demonstrated that young babies have this ability to recognize one, two and three well before they have the language to name numbers. Butterworth's (1999) and Dehaene's (1998) research with brain-injured adults seems to indicate that the ability to subitize is separate from the ability to count. You may have parents at your setting who proudly report of their child's ability to count to three, when in fact the child does not yet under-stand counting, but is merely subitizing.

Numerosity

Numerosity is the ability to compare two collections and say which has more, without counting. There are two factors which affect this: distance and magnitude.

Practical task

Look at Figure 1.1 and decide which side has more, without counting. Do the same with Figure 1.2. Was one easier than the other?

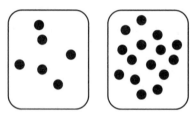

Figure 1.1 Decide which side has more, without counting

⇨

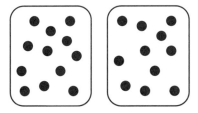

Figure 1.2 Decide which side has more, without counting

The second factor which impacts on numerosity is magnitude, or the size of the numbers. Decide which side has more in Figures 1.3 and Figure 1.4 without counting. Which was easier?

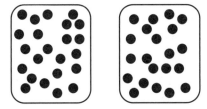

Figure 1.3 Decide which side has more, without counting

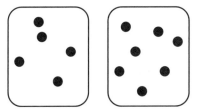

Figure 1.4 Decide which side has more, without counting

In the first set most people will have found Figure 1.1 much easier because the difference between the two numbers, also called the distance, was much larger.

In the second set Figure 1.4 was doubtless easier. In both Figures 1.3 and 1.4 the distance was the same, because the difference between the numbers was two each time but the smaller numbers in Figure 1.4 made it more obvious, even though the numbers were outside the range of subitizing. Although babies have these innate abilities, explicit teaching is needed to build on and extend these skills, bringing them into conscious thought.

Controversy over conservation of number

Piaget's studies of young children have been influential in planning for and teaching in the early years and beyond. Piaget (1952) believed that children could not understand the concepts related to number until they were able to 'conserve'. Piaget's test for conservation of number involved having two identical rows of objects (like marbles or buttons), lined up to emphasize one-to-one correspondence. The child was then asked whether the rows are the same or if one has more. Once the child agrees that they are the same the adult spreads out one of the rows so it extends beyond the other row at both ends. (See Figure 1.5) The child is asked again whether the rows are the same or if one has more. This process can be extended by returning the objects to the one-to-one correspondence and then compressing the row of objects. Piaget found that children below the age of 7 would say that the row which was longer had more. These are children in his 'pre-operational stage' (approximately 2 to 7 years old). He did not think that conservation could be taught which had an impact on teaching approaches in the early years. However, there have been many studies challenging these ideas, a few of which are described below.

Figure 1.5 Are the rows the same?

The assertion that conservation cannot be taught was contradicted by Gelman (1969) who trained 5-year-old children who had previously failed at conservation tasks to recognize that the change was irrelevant and could be ignored in conservation of number and length tasks. They were then more likely to give the correct answers to all conservation tasks, in weight and volume, as well as in number and length.

Mehler and Bever (1967) tested 2-to-4-year-old children but did not try to train them. Instead they altered the test by using different materials. In one of the tests they used marbles in two rows; the one with more marbles was compressed, while the other was spread apart to be longer than the more plentiful row. The children were then asked which row had more. In the alternative version of the test they used M&Ms instead of marbles and the children were allowed to choose one row to eat. The vast majority of children chose the row with more M&Ms. This could mean that the motivation in answering the question was important, but it could also mean that the question itself in the original version caused problems. One particularly interesting finding in this study was that the 2-year-old children were able to conserve in both versions, while the 3-and 4-year-old children could not conserve in the Piagetian version.

Probably the best known challenge to Piaget in the United Kingdom came from Margaret Donaldson. McGarrigle and Donaldson (1974) performed several studies exploring children's understanding of conservation tasks. In one they used a 'naughty teddy' who messed up the neat one-to-one correspondence rows while the adult was not looking. After the rows had been messed up so that one was more spread out than the other, the exasperated adult would ask if the rows were the same or if one had more. In this version around 70 per cent of the 4-to-6-year-olds were able to answer correctly and then were able to answer correctly again when the traditional version of the task was performed later. In discussing this and several other related studies, Donaldson (1978) suggests that this is not the lack of ability to decentre that impacts on conservation tasks, but children's interpretations of the situation and the questioning.

Dehaene (1997) believes that the results of the M&M and naughty teddy studies indicates that Piaget's conservation test does not actually test the child's understanding of number but rather tests the child's theory of mind, their understanding that other people might know and think differently from themselves. By this he meant that the children were changing their answers because in the conventions of questioning you do not ask the same question twice in a row if the answer is the same.

These are not new studies but their inclusion here is important because Piaget's ideas about mathematics have had a powerful, lasting impact. In the early 1990s the National Curriculum for mathematics included testing Key Stage 1 children for their ability to conserve. I have vivid memories of asking one 7-year-old after another whether there was more water, less water or the same amount after pouring from a tall, thin cylinder into a short, wide jug. The children would look at me strangely and then say 'the same' with doubt in their voices. Only one child believed the amount had changed. In the same period, mathematics in nursery and reception classes was dominated by grouping objects into sets and other 'pre-number' activities because young children were believed to be unable to comprehend numbers before they could conserve. This has now changed and there is much more emphasis on number and counting in early years classrooms today. However, Price (2004) has found that many teachers who were trained with Piagetian ideas are uncomfortable with the changed curriculum and do not fully understand the ideas behind it.

Counting

Counting is the basis of most mathematics. The calculations that children learn to do with addition, subtraction, multiplication and division are essentially faster ways of counting. Data handling is all about counting responses and finding ways to represent these. Shape may seem more removed from counting, but a fundamental property of shapes is the number of sides they have. The subitizing and numerosity discussed above are precursors to counting but in order to say that a child can count, much more needs to be present. Counting is a complex matter, much more so than most adults realize.

Photograph 1.1 Counting money (© P. Hopkins)

The different aspects of counting were analysed by Gelman and Gallistel (1978). These are:

- Stable order
- One-to-one correspondence
- Cardinality
- Abstraction
- Order-irrelevance

Stable order

Stable order means that the children learn to say the number names in order. Most parents or carers will teach their children the number names and this is the aspect that many associate most closely with counting. I have had a parent come to me saying that their child in Reception can count to 20, which meant that the child could say the number words in order to 20, but in fact this particular child had not yet mastered the other aspects of counting. It is quite common for young children to miss out a number name when they are first learning them.

Case study

The Foundation unit has children from 3 to 5 years old. They provide many opportunities for counting. At the beginning of each session the children put their photographs on the board. The adult records these in the register and then leads the children in counting how many children are present. Children help prepare and distribute fruit and drinks at snack time and are encouraged to count to see if there are enough. In the outdoor area there is a hopscotch and a number line painted on the ground. Some areas, like the water tray, have a sign and bands indicating the maximum number of children allowed at one time. The adults made observations of the children counting spontaneously, as well as during teacher-led counting activities. Three-year-old Olivia counted one, two, three, four, six, seven, eight, nine, ten but consistently left out the number five, although she could identify the numeral 5 and would answer five if presented with five objects. Alisa, 3 1/2 years old, did not have a stable order when counting. In the first observation she counted one, two, seven, five, three, one, four, two, one. In the second observation she counted one, two, four, two, seven, five, one. Four-year-old Ruben had previously been assessed as being secure in counting to ten. He was now starting to count up to 15 but

---

Case study—Cont'd

frequently missed out the number 8 and called 11 'eleventeen'. At 5 years old Sam was learning to count past 10 but would end up in a little loop saying . . . 8, 9, 10, 11, 12, 13, 14, 6, 7, 8, 9, 10, 11.

Reflection for early career professional

- What do these observations tell you about the children's counting abilities?
- What would you do to move each child forward?

Reflection for leader/manager

- How many observations do you need to make before you consider an assessment judgement to be secure?
- How do you record when a child falters over something where you had previously assessed him/her as being secure?

One-to-One correspondence

One-to-one correspondence is an important aspect of counting and was the focus of Piaget's conservation tests. Although, as demonstrated above, doubt has been cast upon Piaget's conservation tests and whether this is a vital precursor to mathematics, there is no doubt that one-to-one correspondence is an integral part of counting. One-to-one correspondence means that the child matches a different number name to each object. Most of the errors that you encounter with counting will relate to this aspect. Often when children are counting they say the number names faster than they touch the objects. This results in a higher number. Of course, there may be times when saying the number names is slower than the counting, giving the opposite result. Sometimes children miss out an item, resulting in a lower number. Both of these errors can occur whether the thing to be counted is an object, movement or sound. The next error occurs when children cannot remember which have been counted already so they end up counting some of them more than once. This is a particular problem when the objects are arranged in a loop or are very scattered with no discernable pattern. Some problems which appear to be related to one-to-one correspondence are actually problems with stable order, with the child missing out number names or repeating them.

Cardinality

As discussed in the introduction, cardinality is understanding that the final number in the count tells us how many there are in the set. This seems obvious to adults but is less obvious to children. Especially if the parent or carer's emphasis has been on saying the number names in the correct order, the child may understand counting as the process of reciting the words without realizing that there is an underlying goal. A child who does not understand cardinality may simply look confused when asked 'How many are there?' after counting the objects or may respond by going through the whole counting process again.

Munn (1997) studied counting with Scottish children who were finishing nursery. She asked the children if they could count, to which they responded by reciting the numbers (stable order). The next question asked the children to count a collection of blocks (one–to-one correspondence). Then they were asked to give the researcher a certain number of blocks (cardinality). However, the most interesting aspect of her research was when she asked children why they counted. Most of the children counted just because they wanted to or because they wanted to please their parents. Some viewed counting as a way to learn their numbers. The least common category was counting to know how many of something there was, which may be why some children have trouble understanding cardinality. If you think about the daily life of young children they have little need for functional counting because most of their needs are met by the parent or carer. While counting the stairs is good for practising the number sequence, the final number does not really hold any significance. However, you can build opportunities for the cardinal sense of number, for example, asking how many pieces the toast should be cut into.

Case study

When I'm brushing Pippa's hair I give her the option of choosing how many pony-tails to have. She may look slightly odd with five but that was the choice of the day. She is aware that she needs five hair elastics that she takes from the pot and knows that her hair will be divided into five clumps which she can count in the mirror. At bedtime we negotiate the number of stories to be read. She usually opens the bidding with five and I counter with two. The final compromise is generally three. This is a situation in which the cardinality holds a real significance for her.

Case study—Cont'd

Reflection for early career professional

- What counting opportunities do you provide that have a real cardinal significance for the children?

Reflection for leader/manager

- What choices do children get to make in your setting? What are the organi-
  zational implications resulting from allowing choice?

Abstraction and order-irrelevance

The final two aspects, abstraction and order-irrelevance are more abstract, as implied by one of the names. Abstraction is the idea that we can count anything. It may be a very straightforward set, such as the number of eggs in a box. The set may be focused on certain parts, like in pub cricket. The Horse and Rider have six legs altogether. However, the set that we are counting may consist of a random collection, such as the number of things on the table, where the only property they share is the fact that they are on the table. This is a fairly sophisticated concept but one that we take for granted as adults. You can help children with this by providing different collections of objects to count. You can also ask them to show you five (or any other number) and then take turns coming up with different ways to show the number five, including sets of five objects, shapes with five sides, five fingers, the numeral 5, five tally marks, etc. Order-irrelevance means that no matter which object you start with and which order you count them in, you will always end up with the same final number, as long as you count each object once.

Once these five aspects of counting are mastered the child can truly be said to count. However, counting does not stop there. Children need to be able to count forwards and backwards, in different groupings and from different start-ing points. It develops into part numbers such as fractions and ratios. Some-times we do not need to know the specific number so we need to know about rounding and estimating. As numbers get bigger and smaller we need to know

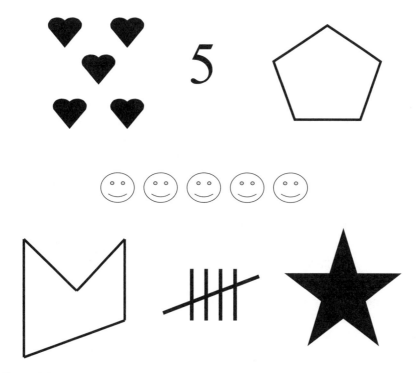

Figure 1.6 Showing 5

about place value, partitioning, decimal numbers and negative numbers. The following sections of this chapter will demonstrate how to develop the ideas and skills related to early number.

Number from birth to 3 years of age

As explained above, babies have some innate number sense but it is difficult to discern this until the babies become mobile and develop language skills. In the first year babies are becoming more and more aware of the world around them. Exploring objects with their hands and mouths helps them to understand the properties of those objects and to recognize that these objects are discrete and separate from themselves (Post and Hohmann, 2000: 37). Recognizing that some things are 'mine' and some things are not helps develop one-to-one correspondence (DCSF, 2008). Noticing movement and changes to sounds and images will help them count those things in the future.

Focusing on body parts can help develop the cardinality of one and two, with one nose, one mouth, one head, two eyes, two ears, two arms, two legs, but will also help develop the abstraction principle that we can count anything. At 23 months Freya was able to transfer this counting of her own body parts to counting two eyes and two ears on her toy hedgehog. She was then able to move from saying bus and more bus to saying two buses.

The EYFS, in the Unique Child theme, recognizes that children develop at varying rates (DCSF, 2008). One area in which there is a large variation is the rate at which children develop expressive language, although most children will start speaking between their first and second birthdays (Johnston and Nahmad-Williams, 2009: 153). Many of the EYFS statements (DCSF, 2008: 63–64) for the birth to 3 years old age group relate to mathematical language, reflecting this linguistic development:

- Develop an awareness of number names through their enjoyment of action rhymes and songs that relate to their experience of numbers (8–20 months)
- Say some counting words randomly (16–26 months)
- Distinguish between quantities, recognizing that a group of objects is more than one (16–26 months)
- Gain awareness of one-to-one correspondence through categorizing belongings, starting with mine or Mummy's (16–26 months)
- Have some understanding of one and two, especially when the number is important for them (22–36 months)
- Use some number language, such as more and a lot (22–36 months)
- Recite some number names in sequence (22–36 months)

Before children can use language themselves, carers should be using mathematical language with them, such as number names, terms like more and less, big and small. More, again and all gone are among the early words that children say, especially when referring to food. This matches the studies with babies and animals mentioned at the beginning of the chapter that found numerosity, the understanding of which was more, developed around 15 to 18 months in babies and was particularly strong in animals in relation to food. Providing small amounts of food and then asking if the child wants more is a way of encouraging this development.

Children start to use number names a bit later, between 18 months and 3 years. Some number rhymes will help introduce the number names just as a sequence, such as:

- One, two, buckle my shoe;
- One, two, three, four, five once I caught a fish alive;
- This old man.

While others develop more of the concepts related to counting, such as:

- Two little dickie birds;
- Five Fat Peas;
- Five Little Monkeys jumping on the bed;
- Five Little Monkeys sitting in a tree;
- Five currant buns;
- Five little men in a flying saucer;
- Five fat sausages;
- There were ten in the bed.

It is no coincidence that so many of the rhymes involve the number five. Initially carers can use their own hands to show the numbers and model taking them away. Gradually children will be able to copy the hand shape and begin to relate the numbers in the songs, rhymes and stories. Five is quite easy for children to show because it involves an open hand. Of the other numbers three is the hardest because two fingers need to be folded down and this

Photograph 1.2 Five fingers (© P. Hopkins)

requires considerable dexterity. Three is an important number in many traditional stories that include numbers: Three Little Pigs, Three Billy Goats Gruff, Goldilocks and the Three Bears, although other numbers appear too, such as Snow White and the Seven Dwarfs.

As children move through the toddler stage they become more interested in the fact that they are growing up. At 26 months Pippa explained that she was not tiny anymore but now tiny and a half, while 6 months later she decided she was medium. The end of breastfeeding or bottles, moving into pants instead of nappies, becoming confidently mobile and growing tall enough to reach things are significant stages in leaving babyhood behind and becoming a big girl or boy. This leads to an interest in ages and birthdays. Strangers often ask children how old they are, well before the child is old enough to answer this. Ruben liked to interact with his Dora the Explorer DVD and would answer when asked his name but at 27 months did not know what to say when asked his age. His mother answered for him, saying you're two and showing two fingers. By 32 months Ruben was able to tell Dora himself that he was 2 and showed it with his own fingers. Khara was very eager to grow up and be older. At 35 months she was talking about her birthday and had decided that she wanted to be 4 on her next birthday rather than 3. It was hard to convince her that it did not work like that. This desire to be older resulted in her emphasizing that she was 3 and a 1/2, not 3, when she was 40 months. Ages are significant numbers

Photograph 1.3 Train cake (© P. Hopkins)

in our society and become increasingly important to children as they move to the next stage described below. It is interesting to consider what is the age at which we stop wishing we were older and start wishing we were younger.

Case study

Felix's parents play lots of games with him where they build anticipation by counting one, two, three before the event. They count one, two, three before he falls into their arms from the bed or is thrown up in the air. His favourite game is when daddy sits on the arm of the sofa and Felix blows on daddy knocking him onto the sofa. At 23 months old Felix went to a parent and toddler group that had a soft play area and little ball pool. He copied the other children climbing up the steps and jumping into the ball pool. He enjoyed this and did it repeatedly, saying something that sounded like one, two, three before each jump. Later at home Felix jumped from the sofa onto cushions on the floor after counting for himself.

Reflection for early career professional

- What value does this sort of counting have for young children?
- How many of the routines you use with children involve numbers?
- Do you draw attention to the numbers by showing fingers or having the relevant number of objects?

Reflection for leader/manager

- Several of the EYFS statements for numbers up to 36 months relate to expressive language.
- Without the audible counting in the case study above would it be apparent that Felix had internalized this aspect of the counting process?
- How can you ensure that you are assessing children's mathematical understanding if they do not yet have sufficient expressive language?

Number from 3 to 5 years of age

At this age the emphasis in number is moving beyond the numbers which can be subitized and developing a deeper understanding of all the aspects of counting. The EYFS statements (DCSF, 2008) suggest a gradual progression through these years, counting up to three or four, then to six; then to ten and beyond. However, children should be exposed to larger numbers as well, in speech, in print and in collections of objects. These could include measuring and talking about the children's heights, having the date on display, counting and recording the number of children in the nursery each day.

When counting objects children should be encouraged to touch each object as they count it. If the children actually move each object from one area to another as they count this can help ensure that they count every object once and once only. Pictures are harder to count because they cannot be moved. In order to help children make certain that they count each object once you can provide counters or blocks to place on each picture as it is counted. This has the added bonus that the count can be checked by then removing and counting the counters. Catherine was talking with children who were making their own monsters. She would ask them how many arms the monsters had, how many googly eyes they needed and encourage the children to compare their monsters to each others'. Gelman (2006) found that children's counting was more accurate when they predicted the amount first and then checked it by counting.

Counting movements, especially their own, can highlight difficulties with one-to-one correspondence. Children can get into a rhythm saying the counting words that might not match the speed of the movements, especially if the movements are irregular. You can provide challenges that are both mathematical and physical by asking children how many times they can pass a ball without dropping it, how many times the balloon can be hit before it touches the ground, how many times in a row they can jump. These can be done individually, in pairs, or in groups with an adult supporting the counting process. Sounds provide a different type of counting experience because they cannot be seen and, unless recorded, only exist in the memory after they have occurred. Jatinder sat with a group of children in a Reception class. She asked the children to close their eyes and then she played several beats on the drum. With their eyes still closed she asked them to show her with their fingers how many beats there were. She observed the children while she played the drum and noticed that some children counted while the drum was playing, some listened first and then counted while replaying the sounds in their memory or by drumming on themselves, while one child did both.

To ensure that children are secure with number order it is important to count in a variety of ways, such as counting forwards and backwards. Counting forwards helps the children to develop their understanding of addition, starting with the concept of one more. Counting down helps with the concept of one less and subtraction. Many children find counting down more difficult than counting up so need lots of practice (Wright et al., 2006: 30). As an adult you are probably confident counting in both directions. However, if you try to say the alphabet backwards you are likely to experience some of the difficulties that young children encounter when counting backwards. Luckily many number rhymes and songs involve counting down.

Case study

Aaron taught the song Five fat sausages to his group of 3 and 4-year-olds in the nursery. He had five children pretending to be the sausages and jumping up to go pop and bang. The other children tried to show the right number of fingers for the sausages. They paused between each verse to give the children time to count back two to find the new number and arrange their fingers. When they got to the last sausage that one went pop and then all the children jumped up because the pan itself went bang. They all thought this was very funny. Several of them sang the song on their own throughout the week and some taught it to their parents at home.

Reflection for the early career professional

- What number songs, stories and rhymes do you use with the children?
- What are the advantages and disadvantages of using songs to teach number?

Reflection for leader/manager

- How do you support children with English as an additional language when using songs and rhymes?

So far the examples have focused on numbers below ten. The English language causes problems with the numbers between ten and twenty. According to

Hafeez (1997) 11 and 12were originally abbreviations for 'ten and one left over' and 'ten and two left over' respectively. Many European languages have similar problems, for example, German elf and zwolf (very similar to our 11 and 12) and French onze and douze (similar to our dozen). An exception to this in Europe is modern Welsh which says un deg un (one ten one) and un deg dau (one ten two) (Cockburn and Littler, 2008: 87). The teen numbers also cause problems because of the similar sounds of the – teen and – ty suffixes and the fact that the teen numbers are said in the opposite order in terms of tens and units. For example, some children confuse 17 and 70 when hearing or saying them. They sometimes confuse 17 and 71 when seeing them for similar reasons. Chinese and Japanese have regular counting words which makes it easier for their children to progress through the two digit numbers (Dehaene, 1997: 104). Courtney had been taught the numbers up to the 20s. She then extended these herself, counting 28, 29, 20–10, 20–11, etc. Kevin enjoyed playing with words and at 45 months was exploring numbers beyond 20. After repeating the numbers in the twenties several times he then decided to make up his own words from the things he could see, such as 20-sign, 20-road and 20-grass and leaves. The teaching assistant who was near him started to play along and they then took turns making up new 20 words. This is an example of Supporting Learning as described in the EYFS Positive Relationships theme, with the adult taking their lead from the child and encouraging exploration (DCSF, 2008).

Although the emphasis so far has been on small numbers, it is important to expose children to larger numbers as well. The larger numbers (60 onwards) are more regular in English so it is easier to spot the linguistic patterns in them, and they prepare children for the range of numbers they will experience around them. Kiara was walking with her childminder and told him that the bus going past was the number 65. She did not know how big that number was but did know it was bigger than 6. She had been working on numbers up to 20 in the nursery but they also talked about larger numbers, which helped her recognize this nominal use of number in the environment. Adam looked at a bush covered in little florets and announced that there were millions of flowers on it. Again, he did not have a precise idea of how much a million was but he knew it was a big number. It does not really matter that he did not have a firm understanding of the exact size of the number yet.

Practical task

Try to imagine £1,000,000. You might associate it with winning the lottery or the things you could buy with it. Now try imagining £1,000,000 in pound coins. If you stacked them in your house how much space would they take up? Most adults have no idea but will still feel comfortable using the word million. Making large collections of small items, like coins, buttons or conkers, spreading them out, arranging them and counting them can help children develop a firmer understanding of large numbers. Think about the resources in your setting. What do you have large collections of that you could use to explore large numbers?

As well as counting in ones, children towards the end of this stage will start to count in groups of two, five and ten. Sophie, 62 months, was very excited that Mrs Alford was going to teach her to count in fives to 50 after the holiday. She practised at home with her parents and was able to count up to 105 with their support. She was really proud of earning a sticker for counting up to 100 in 5s in front of the class. This counting in groups of lays the foundations for multiplication.

As well as developing counting and the cardinal use of number, ordinals are increasingly important during this stage. While collaboration is necessary to get along in society, a degree of competitiveness appears to be innate (Johnston and Nahmad-Williams, 2009: 213). This can be seen in Luca calling 'I want to be first!', as he pushes past his brother to get to the door. Ordinals can be developed through races where there are first, second, third etc., taking advantage of this competitiveness. However, ordinals can also link to more collaborative ventures, such as taking turns: Sally will go first and then Liam will be second and Emma will go third. Ordinals can also refer to routines, such as taking the register first, choice time second, whole group time third and snack time fourth. Adult use of the language of ordinals will support the children in their understanding and their ability to use this language themselves.

Case study

Sarah used the story Kipper's Toy Box by Mick Inkpen as the basis for learning related to Communication, Language and Literacy, Problem Solving, Reasoning and Numeracy, Knowledge and Understanding of the World and Personal, Social and Emotional Development, with her Reception class in the summer term. In the story Kipper keeps counting his toys in different ways because the number keeps changing. It turns out that two mice have nibbled through his toy box and moved some of the toys. Sarah led a discussion about why people had toys, the children's favourite toys and where they stored them. She showed them one of her favourite teddies from when she was a child and some of the toys other members of staff and parents had brought in. They compared old and new toys and discussed the differences. Sarah said she wanted to create a toy museum in the classroom with old toys and new toys. This built up over the next week with children bringing in toys from home. They had to decide how to sort the toys to display them and then they made labels with the name of the toy and the approximate year it was made or used. There were art materials provided for children to make pictures of toys, from observation, memory or their imagination.

Sarah had created a toy box of her own, like Kipper's. She collected toys with different properties, heights and weights. Some of the toys, like the stacking cups and the Russian dolls could be counted as a single entity or each individual cup and doll could be counted. She had also made a simple board game with photographs of the toys and included some number books and tapes. After she read the story with the children they discussed the different ways that Kipper had counted and which they felt was the best way. Sarah worked with the children in pairs, finding ways to sort and count the toys. Yusaf started by counting the toys out loud without moving them and ended up missing one. Sarah asked Veronika to check how many there were by counting them in a different way. They came up with different answers so Sarah asked how they were going to know which was right. Yusaf and Veronika talked about it and decided to put number cards with each toy and agreed that the biggest number would tell them how many. While they were talking Sarah started playing with the Russian dolls and left them spread out so when the children counted again they found there were more. At first Veronika looked confused, but Yusaf laughed and said it was all the babies and decided to spread out the stacking cups too. They discovered that they did not have enough number cards for all the extra toys. Sarah asked them what they were going to do to solve this problem. Yusaf thought they should count a different way but Veronika insisted on using the number cards. She decided that they could lay the cards out in order and then match the toys to them, making extra rows when necessary. Yusaf felt he should check so he counted along the rows, touching each one in turn. This time they both got the right answer. Sarah then asked them if they could put the toys in order. Veronika thought they should use height and decided the first one would be the shortest. Yusaf focused in on the stacking cups and put these in order in a line and then by stacking them.

At the end of this stage children should be attaining the Early Learning Goals (DCSF, 2008: 66) and be able to

- say and use number names in order in familiar contexts;
- count reliably up to ten everyday objects;
- recognize numerals one to nine;
- use developing mathematical ideas and methods to solve practical problems.

Reflection for early career professional

- Which uses of number and aspects of counting are represented in this example?
- How does this activity contribute to development of the Early Learning Goals?
- What assessments could you make for Yusaf and Veronika?
- The statement about solving problems is quite broad. Do you think there was evidence of that problem solving in this example?

Reflection for leader/manager

- How do you utilize the different members of your team to ensure sufficient time for observing and assessing individuals or small groups of children?
- How are the assessments that one person makes shared with other members of the team and how do they contribute to the overall planning process?
- How many opportunities do you provide for problem solving and open-ended investigations?

Oftsed (2008) and Williams (2008) both emphasized the need for problem solving opportunities in Early Years and Key Stage 1. Children need to investigate open-ended problems. Ebbutt (2008) instructs teachers to 'stop your meddling' so that children can make their own decisions. For this they need a mathematically rich environment, sufficient time, freedom and resources.

Transition to Key Stage 1 (5 to 7 years of age)

The Williams Review (2008) emphasizes the need for a smooth transition from the EYFS to Key Stage 1. They recommend using the children's Early Years Profile to inform KS1 teachers and ensure that they are building on the children's previous achievements. However, the Williams Review also stated that the teaching approach should aid transition as well. 'Year 1 teachers should be encouraged to increase opportunities for active, independent learning and learning through play, as in the EYFS' (Williams, 2008: 41). This active learning can provide a great support for children in problem solving and there is no reason why this should stop in Year 1 rather than continuing throughout the children's school life. When Freya was 7 she was sitting with her childminder and the other children having a drink. They decided to do 'cheers', clinking glasses with each other. Freya wondered how many clinks there would be if everybody clinked with everybody else. At first she thought there would be twenty clinks because there were five people with four clinks each. Then she realized that she was counting some of the clinks more than once. With some support from the childminder she worked out it was $4 + 3 + 2 + 1 + 0 = 10$ by thinking about each person in turn, starting with herself. She also realized that she could turn it around so she started with Alison and ended with herself and it would give the same answer. This is essentially a well-known investigation known as the Handshake problem, but it emerged from the child's own play and curiosity.

Counting at this stage still needs to be developed. New problems occur as children have to think more about place value rather than remembering a list of numbers. Harry was experimenting with counting and counted up to 202, then played with going forwards and backwards. There was a little uncertainty at times, especially when he wanted to go from 119 to 200 directly and a couple of times when counting forwards or backwards he reversed the starting number so 94 became 49, demonstrating some confusion with place value. There are many resources which can help consolidate the children's mental images of counting and develop understanding of place value, some of which are described in the following section.

A mathematical environment

Children should be given opportunities in a broad range of contexts, both indoors and outdoors, to explore, enjoy, learn, practise and talk about their developing mathematical understanding. Such experiences develop a child's confidence in tackling problem solving, asking probing questions, and pondering and reasoning answers across their learning. Vitally important is ensuring that children's mathematical experiences are fun, meaningful and build confidence.

(Williams, 2008: 34)

The EYFS places great value on providing Enabling Environments, indoors, outdoors and emotionally (DCSF, 2008), which mirrors the Williams recommendation above.

Ofsted (2008) found that the best provision in the EYFS involved a blend of free choice play and focused learning activities. This depended on a mathematically rich environment, both indoors and outdoors, with resources and routines that encouraged mathematical exploration. This was supported by mathematical discussions between children and adults. Haylock and Cockburn (2008: 9) present a model in which concrete experiences, language, pictures and symbols work together to build cognitive connections. A mathematically rich environment, with supportive practitioners, will include the four elements of this model, rather than letting the symbolic aspect dominate, through an overemphasis on formal recording.

The mathematical environment can involve

- number lines on display
- examples of data handling, such as children's birthdays sorted by month
- maths trails, both indoors and outdoors
- role play and small world opportunities that highlight the mathematics involved
- hopscotch, number tracks and empty ten by ten grids painted on the playground
- timetables showing the daily routine
- digital and analogue clocks
- sand timers
- calendars
- activities labelled for certain number of children, for example, only four children in the sand
- recording the number of children present and absent each day

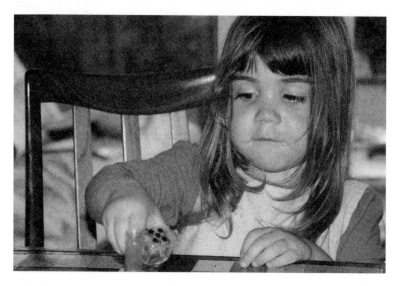

Photograph 1.4 Dice (© P. Hopkins)

One of the examples of 'prime practice' given in the Ofsted (2008) report on mathematics was a role-play toy shop, where children had to choose the price of items and sell them to other children acting as customers. They stated that the process of paying and giving change was an important feature, even though the children were not able to work out the change accurately.

Case study

Julia, Rebecca and Jamie were playing in the toy shop set up in their Nursery class. They had an electric toy till that allowed them to enter numbers and add them up. They enjoyed putting in numbers, although they were random, as was the amount of change given back. After they had played in the toy shop for a while they moved to the toy kitchen area but decided it was a café. They took turns being waitress and customers. As well as writing down orders and delivering food, the waitress presented a bill at the end of the meal and the customers had to pay, again receiving change. There was no till present in the kitchen area so Rebecca went and got a calculator to help work out the money. The children had used their own initiative to transfer their learning to a different context.

Reflection for early career professional

- What other role-play situations involve the use of number?
- What resources would you include to encourage children to use number in their exploration?

Reflection for leader/manager

- It is common with role-play shops (e.g. an apple for 2 p), focusing on numbers that the children can use confidently. Do you think it is more important to keep the numbers realistic or to keep the numbers small? What implications do these have?
- What role-play situations would realistically use small numbers?

In the above example the Information and Communication Technology (ICT) encouraged the children to use numbers and see what happened when they were combined. This sort of use in play is recommended by the Primary Strategy (DCSF, 2009). ICT has considerable potential to extend children's learning (see ICT chapter in KUW book in this series). Unfortunately, Ofsted (2008) found that there was limited use of ICT in mathematics. This may be due in part to confusion about the role of calculators. While ICT is generally seen as a good thing in the curriculum, with the Primary Review (Rose, 2009) recommending it as a core subject across the curriculum, calculators have been viewed with suspicion by parts of the media and government (Compton et al, 2007: 32, 33). Calculators are very useful for exploring place value, number patterns and counting. They can support children in problem solving by allowing them to work with numbers beyond their usual competence and letting children focus on the reasoning rather than the arithmetic.

Mathematical mark making

Worthington and Carruthers (2003) undertook a longitudinal study of children's mathematical mark making in the home and in the nursery class. Initially they were struck by the absence of emphasis on mathematical mark making. Most of the early years professionals they interviewed interpreted children's mark making as early writing or drawing and did not attach mathematical meaning to it. On closer inspection Worthington and Carruthers found that children made a range of marks which carried mathematical meaning. Some of these were drawings to indicate a quantity or a division of quantities. Some were informal tally systems to aid counting, such as lines, dots or ticks. Some children attempted more formal Arabic numerals but these were often difficult to recognize initially. Generally observation of the child and/or discussion with the child was necessary to clarify the mathematical meaning of the marks to the adult.

One day Phillipa, aged 2, was drawing a picture. Her drawing skills and fine motor control were still in the early stage of development so her commentary was necessary for adult interpretation of the picture. She said one, two, three, four, eight, nine, ten as she made the marks. These were her own symbols for the numbers rather than the conventional Arabic numeral or some form of tally and I would not have known she had made marks relating to numbers if I had not talked with her. However, for Phillipa these marks definitely had meaning and she gestured to them several times, consistently using the same counting words with them. She then drew a roundish shape, which she said was a boat, and proceeded to scribble over the page until all was obscured. Hughes (1986) defined a series of categories for representations of number. Phillipa's marks would be described by Hughes as idiosyncratic, the most basic stage. Whereas, Freya, aged 5, had advanced to the symbolic stage, where standard forms of numerals are used. She enjoyed writing numbers and had decided to write the numbers in order on her blackboard. After several days of gradually adding to the list she had made it to 42. In between the idiosyncratic and symbolic stages are pictographic (pictures of the objects), iconic (tallies or some other form of repeated symbol) and written (writing letters and/or words).

Worthington and Carruthers felt that the mathematical marks need to be owned by the child rather than dictated by the adults. To support this they recommend providing both opportunities and encouragement for children to record their mathematical thinking. They need plenty of paper and writing materials and exposure to a range of mathematical marks made by adults and children, including graphs, tables, pictograms, tallies, dice numbers and number lines. Bobby (45 months) found a calendar in the writing area. She copied the numbers one to seven in the calendar squares. She then went on to write the numbers three to ten without a visible model. The calendar provided the inspiration to write numbers and the availability of blank paper and writing materials enabled her to take this further. The Nrich website has an activity called Stone Age Counting that shows some prehistoric marks found in a cave in Spain. This image could provide a focus for a discussion with the children about what these marks represented, what these ancient people could have been counting and why they wanted to record it. The Williams Review (2008) picked up on Carruthers and Worthington's work and recommended Continuing Professional Development (CPD) about children's mathematical mark making for staff and emphasized that children should be encouraged in their mathematical mark making. It should be noted that this does not mean that children should be given a diet of worksheets and be expected to write number sentences from an early age. In fact Worthington and Carruthers (2003) found that where the emphasis was on formal recording, the children struggled with the mathematical concepts compared with those who had been encouraged to make their own marks in their own way.

Practical tasks

Observe your children making marks. Are any of them mathematical? Can you distinguish between mathematical marks and other forms of emergent writing and drawing?

Audit your setting. What sort of mathematical representations are visible? Are there numerals, tally marks, dice patterns, charts, tables and pictograms? Set up some resources or areas to encourage mathematical marking. Discuss mathematical marks with children. Evaluate whether specific resources, role play, small world situations or interactions with children have an impact on the mathematical marks the children are making.

Resources

There are many resources available to support the understanding of number. One of the most important is having interesting objects to count. These can be:

- natural objects (such as shells, stones and feathers)
- everyday manufactured objects (such as buttons, coins and cups)

- toys (such as toy animals, cars and dolls)
- craft materials (such as pipe cleaners, pompoms and googly eyes)
- mathematical resources (such as cubes, Compare Bears and counters).

Having a range of materials to count helps to develop the abstraction principle but also provides an opportunity to personalize learning by responding to children's interests. It is important to consider choking hazards when working with young children, especially under 36 months. Care should be taken with any small objects.

Photograph 1.5 Stones (© P. Hopkins)

Some resources help children develop a mental model of numbers and how they relate to each other. These include:

- Interlocking foam numbers (that the children can walk on)
- Number jigsaw puzzles
- Number tracks (where the numbers are in the spaces)
- Number lines (where the numbers are on the lines and the spaces in between represent fractions/decimals)
- Counting stick (where the divisions can represent any equal spaces)
- Washing line with number cards and pegs

- Cuisenaire rods (the different lengths and colours represent the numbers one to ten)
- Numicon (interlocking plastic shapes with holes where the number of holes represents the number)
- Dienes base 10 apparatus (small unit cubes, sticks for tens, flats for hundreds and large cubes for thousands)
- Calendars
- Hundred squares (either 1–100 or 0–99)
- Arrow cards (to demonstrate partitioning and place value)

The resources on their own do not produce the mental images so the teacher needs to help children with this transition (Askew, 2008). It is important that the resources are linked to practical experiences, discussion and symbolic use of number, following Haylock and Cockburn's (2008) model, in order to embed understanding. In their research Tacon et al. (2004: 7) found that using phrases such as 'let your fingers be your eyes' and 'try to see the shapes in your mind's eye' were helpful in making the link between the resource (Cuisenaire rods and Numicon) and the mental image.

Some resources are useful for generating numbers:

- Dice
- Spinners
- Playing cards
- Digit cards

Many ICT resources support the understanding of number:

- Calculators
- Programmable robots
- Electronic tills
- Toy Automated Teller Machines (ATM)
- Remote controls for televisions
- Clocks and stopwatches
- Computer programs and internet activities designed to develop number

In addition to these resources there are number books, number songs and number games. Ebbutt (2002), who designs number games for education, emphasizes that it is important to evaluate the games and adapt them to suit your children. This may mean having more or fewer players, changing resources, such as spinners to dice, or involving older children initially to help teach the game.

Practical tasks

Audit the resources in your setting to support number. Consider when they are used, how they are accessed and who decides which resource to use. Evaluate the impact specific resources have on different children's mathematical understanding. Include the use of different resources in your planning to personalize children's learning.

Home support for number

The EYFS emphasizes the importance of parents as partners in children's education (DCSF, 2008) and so it is important to consider the opportunities for mathematical development in the home. There are many opportunities to support children's understanding of number in our daily lives and they have the added benefit of involving the children in household routines. Helping with the laundry involves ideas of sets, sorting into different colours and matching, such as finding pairs of socks. Setting the table requires an understanding of one-to-one correspondence in order to match the number of settings to the number of people and develops abstraction since you need to count cutlery, plates, glasses, etc. Sharing food may not only involve counting, but also develops ideas of fractions. You can ask children how they would like their food cut up. You can then discuss that the sandwich is in four quarters or the pizza is in eight pieces. However, it is important for adults to be careful with their use of language. I have frequently heard adults requesting the bigger half when a piece of cake was cut. Children need to understand that there cannot be a 'bigger half' because the definition of half means that both pieces are the same size.

Numerals are all around in the home and on the street. Many children quickly learn which numbers to press on the remote control in order to operate the television. You can draw children's attention to numbers on buildings, signs, buses etc. This can be a good opportunity to introduce the language of larger numbers than the child can count. Children can also explore numbers while helping out with DIY or cooking projects. Allow them to use a tape measure, ask them to help you read the scales or the line on the measuring jug. Get them to look at the clock to help you time one minute for whipping the batter.

There are many books, songs and rhymes which focus on counting, often counting down. Adults should model one-to-one correspondence by touching the pictures while counting and then encourage the child to do the same. These books usually have the numeral prominently displayed so the adult can emphasize the link between the number of objects and the numeral. Most board games involve counting, recognizing numbers from a spinner, card or dice and then moving a counter the appropriate number of squares. Snakes and Ladders often goes up to 100 so helps to develop counting with larger numbers. One potentially confusing aspect of Snakes and Ladders is that the path zig zags up the board, whereas children used to a hundred square from school will be used to the numbers consistently increasing from left to right. Both dice and cards help children develop mental images of numbers through their fixed arrangements of spots or symbols. Games like Yahtzee, Cribbage, and Shut the box are great for developing calculation skills but simpler games like Snap help with number recognition. Ofsted (2008) suggests having a maths games library where parents can borrow maths games to play with their children at home. These can be traditional games, like those described above, or can be specially designed games to meet specific objectives in the curriculum.

Case study

The Robertson family likes the anticipation of Advent and the excitement leading up to the Christmas period. As their children have grown they have developed a series of family traditions to help them celebrate. They have a cloth Advent calendar with numbered pockets where they place a little sweet or present each day. They have a wooden board with numbered characters from the Christmas story. One is put on the board each day, progressively building up the scene. They have a nativity set which they use to re-enact the Christmas story, gradually moving the characters around the house, from the angel Gabriel telling Mary she is going to have a baby to the three magi arriving with gifts for the new baby. In addition to these there is

⇨

Case study—Cont'd

a candle ring, with an additional candle lit each Sunday and a numbered candle burned daily. These resources give the children a very real context and purpose for identifying the numbers 1 to 24. This extension into the 20s is quite significant since most counting materials for young children stop at 10, or at most 20. The resources also invite calculations, such as how many more days until Christmas and how many days until we can burn the candle again since we forgot it and let it burn too much yesterday. Sophie really started to take an interest in the numbers when she was about 3 1/2. Each year she has grown more confident with them and now helps her little brother Ben to find the right one each day.

Having put so much effort into the Advent season the Robertsons do not want Christmas to be all over in a day, with the great sense of let down that can entail. Instead they keep going through the 12 days of Christmas. On Christmas day they sort out the presents and select one to be opened on each of the 12 days of Christmas. Mum and dad rarely have enough to last the whole period so they spread theirs out but so far the children have acquired at least 12 each. Sophie and her friend Aisha made some Christmas decorations with the numbers 1 to 12 on them. These are attached to the relevant presents on Christmas day and then transferred to the tree each day. In addition to the mathematical benefits, there are considerable social and emotional benefits because the frenzied Christmas day present opening is avoided. The children have the chance to appreciate each present separately and have time to write a thank you letter each day.

Reflection for early career professional

- What seasonal celebrations do you have in your setting? Have you considered the possibilities for number within them?
- If you do plan activities about Christmas or other religious festivals, in what way do you take into account that some families might not celebrate these because of their own cultural or religious beliefs?

Reflection for leader/manager

- How can you find out about the various traditions your children's families have?
- Would it be appropriate to share some of these traditions with all of the families, with suggestions on how to maximize learning opportunities within them?
- How can you help parents and carers to recognize and use opportunities for number in the home?

Conclusion

Number is an important part of our lives, as labels, indicating order and for counting, and provides the basis for arithmetic. Children experience number and have some understanding of it from birth but we need to provide a mathematically rich environment, in which we encourage exploration and experimentation, to help children develop a deeper understanding of this important aspect of mathematics.

References

Antell, S. and Keating, D. (1983), 'Perception of numeric invariance in neonates', *Child Development*, 54, 695–701

Askew, M. (2008), 'They're counting on us', *Teach Primary*, (July) 48–49

Boysen, S. and Capaldi, E. (eds) (1993), *The Development of Numerical Competence: Animal and Human Models*. Hillsdale, NJ: Erlbaum

Butterworth, B. (1999), *The Mathematical Brain*. London: Macmillan

Cockburn, A. and Littler, G. (2008), *Mathematical Misconceptions*. London: Sage

Compton, A., Fielding, H. and Scott, M. (2007), *Supporting Numeracy*. London: Paul Chapman Publishing

DCSF (2008), *Practice Guidance for the Early Years Foundation Stage*. London: Department for Children, Schools and Families

DCSF (2009), *The Use of Calculators in the Teaching and Learning of Mathematics* [on-line http:// nationalstrategies.standards.dcsf.gov.uk/node/19432?uc=force_uj]

Dehaene, S. (1997), *The Number Sense*. Oxford: Oxford University Press

Donaldson, M. (1978), *Children's Minds*. London: Fontana Press

Ebbutt, S. (2002), 'The importance of trialling', *Mathematics Teaching*, 178, (March), 32–33

Ebbutt, S. (2008), 'Stop your meddling', *Teach Primary*, September, 1–2

Gelman, R. (1969), 'Conservation acquisition: A problem of learning to attend to relevant attributes', *Journal of Experimental Child Psychology*, 7, 167–187

Gelman, R. (2006), 'Young natural-number arithmeticians', *Current Directions in Psychological Science*, 15, (4), 193–197

Gelman, R. and Gallistel, C. R. (1978), *The Child's Understanding of Number*. Cambridge, MA: Harvard University Press

Hafeez, R. (1997), 'Introduction', in Mosley, F. (ed.) *Big Numbers*. London: BEAM

Hauser, M. (2000), 'What do animals think about numbers?', *American Scientist*, 88, (2), 144–149

Haylock, D. and Cockburn, A. (2008), *Understanding Mathematics for Young Children*. London: Sage

Hughes, M. (1986), *Children and Number*. Oxford: Blackwell

Inkpen, M. (2008), *Kipper's Toybox*. London: Hodder Children's Books

Koechlin, E, Dehaene, S. and Mehler, J. (1997), 'Numerical representations in five-month-old human infants', *Mathematical Cognition*, 3, 89–104

Johnston, J. and Nahmad-Williams, L. (2009), *Early Childhood Studies*. Harlow: Pearson Education Ltd.

Matsuzawa, T. (1985), 'Use of numbers by a chimpanzee', *Nature*, 315, 57–59

McGarrigle, J. and Donaldson, M, (1974), 'Conservation accidents'. *Cognition*, 3, 341–350

Mehler, J. and Bever, T. (1967), 'Cognitive capacity of very young children'. *Science*, 158, 141–142

Munn, P. (1997), 'Children's beliefs about counting', in Thompson, I. (1997) *Teaching and Learning Early Number*. Buckingham: Open University Press

Office for Standards in Education (2008), *Mathematics: Understanding the Score*. London: OFSTED

Pepperberg, I. (1987), 'Evidence for conceptual quantitative abilities in the African grey parrot: Labeling of cardinal sets,' *Ethnology*, 75, 37–61

Piaget, J. (1952), *The Child's Conception of Number*. London: Routledge and Kegan Paul

Post, J. and Hohmann, M. (2000), *Tender Care and Early Learning*. Ypsilanti, MI: High/Scope Educational Research Foundation

Price, A. (2004), 'Is it time to let go of conservation of number?' *The 28th International Conference of the International Group for the Psychology of Mathematics Education*. 14–18 July 2004. [on-line http://www.emis.de/proceedings/PME28/SO/SO079_Price.pdf]

Rose, J. (2009), *Independent Review of the Primary Curriculum: Final Report*. Nottingham: DCSF

Strauss, M. and Curtis, L. (1981), 'Infant perception of numerosity', *Child Development*, 52, 1146–1152

Tacon, R., Atkinson, R. and Wing, T. (2004), *Learning about Numbers with Patterns*. London: BEAM Education Research Papers

Williams, P. (2008), *Independent Review of Mathematics Teaching in Early Years Settings and Primary Schools*. Nottingham: DCSF

Wright, R., Stanger, G., Stafford, A. and Martland, J. (2006), *Teaching Number in the Classroom with 4–8 year olds*. London: Sage

Wynn, K. (1996), 'Infants' individuation and enumeration of actions', *Psychological Science*, 7, 164–169

Worthington, M. and Carruthers, E. (2003), *Children's Mathematics: Making Marks, Making Meaning*. London: Paul Chapman Publishers

Calculating

Introduction: calculating in the early years

Calculating is used here in a broad sense to indicate the application of mathematical reasoning to any situation. This includes, but is not limited to, using numbers to complete 'sums'. Calculating in the early years involves children in making connections in their minds (Haylock and Cockburn, 2003), making generalizations, recognizing patterns and sequences, grouping and sorting and solving problems (DCSF, 2008). When children make connections between objects, groups of object, pictures, experiences and language, they are developing understandings (Haylock and Cockburn, 2003) and beginning to calculate. For example, children understand that extra food added to their plate at meal times 'equals' more food, although 'less' is a much more elusive concept and infrequent word in children's vocabulary (Walkerdine, 1988). Children may notice that a toy train gets longer when we add carriages to it, or the pattern on a calendar where all Sundays are coloured red. They may recognize that adding water to their bath makes it '*more full*'. When children sort a collection of objects, they identify similarities and differences between them and may notice that one group is larger than another and are thus calculating.

Children understand when we sing number and action songs what the language of number relates to; children may hold up three fingers when they hear the word '*three*' or connect the word to the numeral. Songs can thus support early number calculations in the form of abstractions of counting usually to predict +/–1 or +/–2. When children identify patterns in size, number, shape, they are also calculating. Freya (39 months) responded to being told there were 10 minutes left, by saying that this was 4 minutes and 6 more minutes. The calculation had no obvious purpose but showed an ability to relate number facts to different situations. When children solve simple social problems, such as how to share a bag of sweets or an apple within a group, they are also calculating. Though sometimes social conventions and number conventions conflict: Douane (6 years old) was shown a picture of two dogs and asked how many there were and how many there would be if one was taken away. He had no difficulty identifying that there were two dogs, even though one was clearly just a puppy. But the second question posed a real life problem. He looked carefully at the picture and asked plaintively: '*But which dog?*' He was all too aware that taking the adult dog away might soon '*take away*' the puppy too. At this point, his understanding of animal husbandry was stronger than his understanding of the conventions of textbook calculations.

Thus in myriad simple ways calculating occurs throughout our lives and, as we will see in the following sections, there is much evidence to suggest that it begins even before children learn to walk and talk.

The development of calculating

Mathematical reasoning is powerful in allowing us to move between particular examples to certainties we cannot see. Effective calculating is when we can *see* the certainty. An expectation for pupils achieving level 2 in the national curriculum is that they should be able to '*explain why an answer is correct*' (DfEE, 1999b: 9) and this deceptively simple phrase captures much of what calculating is about. It is not a matter of simply getting correct answers, but of knowing that, and explaining why, the answer must be correct.

An early Standard Assessment Task (SAT) for children of 6 and 7 required them to add single digit numerals on two dice quickly and without visibly counting. They were thus meant to demonstrate that they *knew* the number bonds as facts. I explored this activity with many children up to seven and also with adults – including some highly competent mathematicians. It was obvious that all knew at least some of these number facts by the instant recall that was expected. It was equally obvious that most actually calculated some of the number pairs during the task. Some could be seen using their fingers to count, or to chunk and manipulate the numbers in some way. Some would stare at an invisible array of counters on the table between us conjuring up a number pattern they could handle (subitizing). Others, when asked, would generate the unknown sum from a known number bond, for example: '*I know two fives are ten, so three and five is two less, that's eight.*' I also provided dice with different numerals (Chinese, Arabic, or random spots etc.) in order to put the adults into the position of children who may themselves be unsure of the meaning of a specific numeral. The result was to slow down the response rate and to increase the use of fingers to 'hold' one of the numbers. In terms of the standard assessment task, only those who recognized and knew the bonds would be deemed successful. However, many of the others showed successful and ingenious use of calculating strategies. Moreover their certainty in a calculated answer might well outlive the certainty in a recalled fact because the very process of calculation would allow them to '*explain why the answer is correct*'. The main strategies used were counting on, when one number was small; chunking and manipulating the numbers into fives and tens when numbers were larger, and adjusting a random known number bond to provide the required calculation.

The last 25 years have seen considerable interest in exploring the abilities of young children in solving problems and calculating. Some of this stems from unsettling evidence indicating that children can demonstrate strong mathematical abilities at home or in the wider world which then seem to disappear or regress once they are in a formal early years settings. For example Tizard and Hughes (1984) recorded 3-and-4-year-olds both in their homes and in nurseries contrasting some rich and exploratory mathematical dialogue at home with trite interrogations of children in nurseries. A similar stark contrast is reported by Nunes and Bryant (1996) working with older children. Here the group scrutinized were young street vendors in Brazil.

These youngsters were very reliable in their calculations when trading, but had considerably more difficulty in completing exactly the same transactions presented as word problems or computation exercises. We need to be aware that the mathematical opportunities provided in early learning settings may simply not be eliciting or extending children's abilities, as exhibited in other situations.

Hughes seminal work (Hughes, 1986) with its exploration of children's natural mathematics in game like situations, is important here. In his 'Box Test', based on observing a 4-year-old during spontaneous play, Hughes began to use a box and invite children to say how many bricks were in it as they watched the researcher adding some, or taking some out. Later the researcher simply said what was done, the bricks and the box were not visible. When there were up to three bricks, many 2 and 3-year-olds were successful, even though they could not see, and did not want, the contents. However, only by four could they confidently begin to handle numbers greater than three including some precise and certain calculating statements such as this one from Richard (aged 57 months) *'You just have to put one in . . . and then you can take three out'* (Hughes, 1986: 27). Formal abstract presentation (*'How many is three and one more?'*) and the use of standard symbols, especially those for operations, were barriers to calculation. Although young children's ready success was with very small numbers and real or hypothetical situations, this research none the less demonstrates that many young children can abstract and calculate with certainty in familiar contexts from an early age.

This contrasts with the use of Piaget's model of children's thinking (Piaget, 1950) that has dominated the organization of the teaching of mathematics in England for 50 years or more (see previous chapter, Compton, 2010). The influence of Piaget's cognitive theory and symbolic representation on our understanding of calculating is recognized (Scottish Consultative Council on the Curriculum, 2003). However, the consequence of adopting a cognitive model that stresses what children cannot do, has been to limit the expectations we have of them in formal settings and consequently to constrain their skills. Traditionally much of the mathematical work in nursery and reception classes is aimed at eliciting whether or not children can 'conserve number' before they are expected, or even allowed, to count or use numbers in context. Activities typically involve sorting, comparing and ordering sets of very small quantities and recognizing standard numerals. Activities which involve counting or calculating are limited. The Durham project (reported in Aubrey, 1997) which followed seven reception teachers for a full year, found no evidence of practical problem solving work in over half the classes, and very little in the others.

Other educators have used rather different interpretations of Piaget leading to approaches to early mathematics that involve children in making their own decisions about what to do and how to record it. Kamii takes a constructivist approach and talks of young children 're-inventing arithmetic' as they explore number through games (Kamii, 1989). Bird (1991) worked with a reception class encouraging them to take '*an active thinking approach*' to mathematics and deciding both what to do and how to do it. Atkinson (1992) reports a number of approaches that build on Hughes' work and encouraged children to develop their own recording system for numbers, thus coining the phrase '*emergent mathematics*' as a parallel to emergent writing (Hall, 1989).

A rather more specialized approach was taken by the CAN (Calculator Aware Number) project which ran from 1986–89 in which children had unrestricted access to calculators and were encouraged to record their calculations in their own styles. An underlying principal of the project was that '*children should be allowed to use calculators in the same way that adults use them: at their own choice, whenever they wish to do so*' (Shuard et al., 1991: 7). Although the main target group were 6-year-olds at the start of the project, in several project schools children were encouraged to use calculators in imaginative and structured play in nursery and reception classes too. This allowed them to model numerals and operation symbols through both free play and guided explorations from a very early age. Through the use of calculators the number system itself becomes an object of investigation. Pupils generated large numbers, zero, decimals and negative numbers much sooner than they would have encountered them in structured textbooks. However, the context of the calculator allowed them to explore the meaning of these numbers, rather than ignore them. Thus children halving numbers will soon accept that 0.5 is the way the calculator writes a half, even though they will not realize that it does so because a half is equivalent to five tenths.

A key point in these approaches is to encourage children to talk about their mathematical reasoning and decision making, rather than just to strive for correct answers and count the ticks they get! To achieve this would necessitate a shift in the adult's role from prescribing maths activities and scripting maths talk to listening and responding to children's words as they grapple with calculation. One teacher in the CAN project summed up this change *'Role reversal is the best description of my re-thinking. I gradually became an adviser and listener rather than an instructor. I became the learner, the children the teachers. May mind was opened to new approaches, new ideas, new concepts. I began to realise that my way was not necessarily the only correct way'* (Shuard et al., 1991, 45).

However, despite wide reporting of these projects to enhance children's spontaneous and extended use of maths, and the increased role for sharing methods embedded in the national strategies, worksheets still dominate many settings. Worthington and Carruthers (2003) report a survey of 273 teachers which showed that all the classes of Key Stage 1 and 2 children used worksheets for mathematics and so did the reception classes and 20 per cent of nurseries. Yet these stylized and symbolic presentations may actually deter rather than encourage the spontaneous calculations and mathematical thinking that children can do. The following sections suggest some alternative activities that may enrich the maths talk and opportunities for calculation in different settings.

Calculating from birth to 3 years of age

We often underestimate the ability of babies and young children in a range of areas of development and this includes their ability to calculate. Jordan and Brannon (2006) indicate that young children have a grasp of mathematics and mathematical skills at a very early age, before they even learn to walk and talk. In their research they found that by the age of seven months children are able to match the number of voices they hear with the number of faces they see and are thus able to abstract. Other research (BBC, 2009) has shown that babies spend more time looking at number puzzles that they cannot understand, than at those that make sense to them. With reference to the research by Jordan and Brannon (2006), *Dr Anna Franklin of the Surrey Baby Lab, Department of Psychology, University of Surrey, UK, told the BBC News website.*

'The findings support the argument that young infants are capable of a wide range of mental operations and that infants are smarter than we think" (BBC, 2006: 1). Pound (2006) notes that young children are 'persistent problem solvers' and that many spontaneous activities involve recognizing small numbers and identifying changes. For example, a simple game that can intrigue and delight babies is to show them three toys which are then covered with a blanket. Sometimes, not always, a toy is moved, removed or added before the blanket is removed. Although the babies cannot speak they can exhibit intrigue and delight at these simple changes.

So young children are able to think logically and understand the existence of objects and the number of objects even when they are out of their sight. The more stimulation they receive and the more motivating experiences they have, the greater the opportunities for their mathematical development (see Griffiths, 1988). At this early age, children learn by observing and practising. They sort and group objects, arrange things in order and according to their properties. They make comparisons between objects, remove and add to groups and begin to count. Each child develops differently. Trundley (2008)

Photograph 2.1 Young children observing and sorting

contrasted the growing number confidence of her twin daughters between the ages of 18 months and 5 years. While Emily readily learned the number rhyme and could soon count impressively, Alice made a slower start but more secure progress. Trundley attributes this to the Alice's ability to visualize and subitize numbers recognizing that 3 was two and one more, or that five could be split into two and two and one. Ideally, of course, the two skills need to go together and children should be encouraged to use numbers in their talk. For example, Freya, aged 25 months, counted three people in the garden, and was then able to add Grandma and say '*four*'. Her counting was not always reliable but it had purpose and supported calculation of 'one more'.

Many toys for children under 3 years of age, support their mathematical development and ability to calculate. Activity tables and mats allow children to sort and group objects; toy work benches enable children to see where objects are stored and when missing, thus enabling them to calculate what and how many objects are missing. Trucks or wheel barrows of bricks can similarly enable children to pack the bricks into the space and calculate how many are missing. Other toys involve putting shapes or coloured objects into slots and this too encourages children to sort, match and count.

Number rhymes and stories enable children to count and add or subtract small numbers in a fun way and encourage mental calculations. Dice and spinners with 1, 2, 3 spots can be used to indicate moves on a board. Other games, such as picture pairs, snap, build a body or magnetic fishing can also encourage calculation. For example, while playing a magnetic fishing game, children can work out who has the most fish, how many are left in the pond and how many more they need to win. Children can be encouraged to calculate with these small numbers using, for example, Hughes' Box Game; they can calculate the number when one has been added or subtracted and also record this in their own way.

The key aspects of calculating that you are supporting from birth to 3 are:

- Matching, sorting and noticing change;
- Using counting to predict +/−1;
- Subitizing small numbers to recognize that, say, four is made up of two twos;
- Developing a personal recording system of notation through 'emergent maths'.

Case study

A collection of stuffed toy animals (rabbit, mouse, hedgehog, dog, cat), pull along animals (dog, caterpillar) and a rocking and hobby horse were put into a 'pet shop' area so that children could play with them, buy and sell them and care for them in a role-play situation. The learning outcomes were many with aspects of social development (cooperation with others), knowledge and understanding of the world (understanding of the physical needs of animals) as well as mathematic development (calculating). A separate creative activity involved the children making animals using playdough or modelling clay and straws, pipe-cleaners etc. (see de Bóo, 2004).

Reflection for early career professional

- What calculating opportunities are there in these activities for children up to 3 years of age?
- How could you support and challenge children in this activity to develop calculating skills?
- What activities do you currently use that provide opportunities for calculating?
- How could you further develop calculating opportunities in your classroom?

Reflection for leader/manager

- Undertake an audit of activities in your setting over one day that would develop calculating skills.
- How are the different activities differentiated to support less able children and challenge the more able children?
- How can you increase and enhance opportunities for calculating in your setting for all children?

Calculating from 3 to 5 years of age

From about 3 years of age children will begin to compare two groups of objects and recognize when they have the same or different number of objects. This may still be a challenge for them at first as their perceptions of number may not reliably lead them to conserve number in all situations. We do need to be careful not to underestimate what children are capable of as they appear to be able to solve mental calculations and recognize patterns in their calculations from an early age (Haylock and Cockburn, 2003). One important feature of this age group is that they will increasingly work cooperatively as well as individually and this provides new scope for exploiting games and investigations mathematically. Early years settings thus have a crucial role in encouraging children to explore and relish number alongside all their other explorations of, for example, painting, physical activity or the outside world.

Case study

In one play context, Jimmy (4), was putting small pompom balls into two plastic beakers; one short and wide and one tall and thin. He counted the number he put into one beaker and then put the same number into the other. This puzzled him and he spent a few minutes looking at each beaker and then one by one he took out and counted the pompoms in each beaker and then counting them again put them back and finally repeated the activity again. As he did it he mumbled to himself, 'Six, there can't be six in this one – It's got more in it' (looking at the tall thin beaker). After a considerable time, Jimmy said 'There are six in each one – that's very strange.'

Reflection for early career professional

- How could you support Jimmy in an activity such as this?
- How can you extend this activity to challenge him further?
- What other activities can challenge children to show a developing interest in number and calculation?

Reflection for leader/ manager

- How do you plan for challenging problem-solving mathematical activities in your setting?
- Evaluate the use of language by both children and adults engaged in one or more such activity.
- How do you provide the appropriate support and challenge for all children to ensure that they can each develop at an individual rate?
- What activities do you provide for different age groups that can challenge children in their calculations and encourage their exploration of mathematics?

Number problems of different sorts can help children to develop their reasoning abilities and help them to articulate patterns which may become the basis for calculations. For example, children could be challenged to make different shapes with four or five multi-link cubes (see Figure 2.1). In doing this, children will recognize that the total number of cubes is the same however they fix them together. They also have to decide whether or not two arrays are the same: is a vertical tower of five cubes the same as a horizontal rod of five? A harder decision again is to know that all the possible ways of putting five cubes together have been found. Different children may make different decisions, so the ability to explain their reasoning is crucial. Similar problems could include what different ice cream cones or plates of food could be made using a restricted range of ingredients? What different bracelets can be made from a set of beads? How many ways can you colour a flag? (See Bird, 1991, for examples of ways of turning routine activities and worksheets into mathematically rich explorations for this age group.).

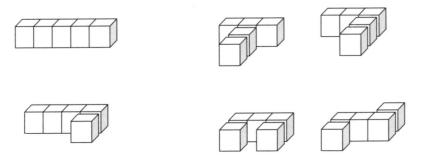

Figure 2.1 Ways to make 5 with multi-link cubes

Application, the ability to apply mathematic understandings in different contexts, is central to calculating and is seen (Hughes et al., 2000) to be a major problem for many children. Relevant practical activities are key to helping children to apply their knowledge and extend their understandings with confidence (Ensing and Spencer, 2003). It is better to place calculating activities into real-life contexts as this is not just more motivating but also helps to make the calculations relevant and easy to comprehend. Such opportunities may abound in role play. For example, is there a note pad in the café for taking orders and calculating bills? Is there a till in the shop and provision for 'paying' by credit card as well as with coins and notes? Are there charts and tables to refer to when servicing different cars in the 'garage'? Opportunities for reasoning and calculation also occur in activities of the classroom itself. For example, how can we organize the snacks so everyone gets a share? How can we make sure that everyone has a chance to use the computer?

Other number problems that involve calculating include:

- Combining two heaps of conkers and estimating how many there will be in total before calculating it
- Sharing a bag of mixed sweets into two or three piles so that each pile has the same number and type of sweet
- Sorting buttons into different groups and calculating how many will be/are in each group
- Explaining to others how they solved a number problem and sharing different ways to solve the same problem
- Calculating how long different sand timers take to finish by counting while the sand falls.

Children can combine, subtract, share and repeat calculations or check them with others. They can compare, talk about their ideas and develop the language of calculating, such as 'add', 'subtract', 'share', 'combine', 'more than', 'less than', 'equals'. Shared practical activities will ensure that children do not just develop skills but also understandings and appropriate vocabulary (Gifford, 2005). Many calculations are dependent on subitizing and recognizing patterns, such as number bonds to make five or counting in twos on a number line or square, or that five is one more than four and one less than six.

Games can provide opportunities for children to practise and repeat number calculations by counting and developing a repertoire of known bonds. The simplest games involve using dice, spinners or cards etc. to show a number which is then added to the total. For example, who can get the highest score throwing two dice? Start with ten counters, pick a number card and discard that many counters, who has the least number of counters now?

Young children can also show an understanding of the number system itself through play situations. Though traditionally we start with numbers to five, ten and twenty, Hughes work (1989) showed that children had a ready understanding of zero – a number often omitted in early calculations. The CAN project also showed how ready access to calculators allowed young children to explore numbers beyond the range they can actually visualize or use. In a reception class children were invited to suggest the biggest number they

Photograph 2.2 Children working with multi-link cubes (photograph by Tracy Gannon, Headteacher, Ripley Infant School)

could and were entranced that their teacher could always give one bigger. The conversation I heard went something like this:

- A million
- A million and one
- One hundred million
- One hundred million and one
- A million billion
- A million billion and one . . .

Although these enormous numbers had little empirical meaning for the children – or indeed the teacher – the opportunity to introduce them into classroom talk and to realize that there was always 'one more' would help the children to understand the number system.

The key aspects of calculating that you are supporting from 3–5 are:

- Using maths in rich role-play contexts and through real life applications
- Developing a sense of pattern, prediction and rules
- Developing confidence in knowing and using random number bonds
- Exploring the number system, with and without a calculator.

Transition to Key Stage 1 (5 to 7 years of age)

The William's Review (2008: 62) of teaching mathematics in the early years has identified 'semantic differences between the way that mathematics is described and construed in the new EYFS framework and in the National Curriculum, which tend to make for discontinuity between the Foundation Stage and Key Stage 1'. These findings reinforce the importance of professional communication between practitioners in the Early Years Foundation Stage and Key Stage 1 settings. Transition is a process and not an event (Johnston and Nahmad-Williams, 2008) and smooth transition requires excellent communication between professionals in both phases of learning (Sanders, et al., 2005; Primary National Strategy, 2006). Williams (2008) also identified a problem with pedagogical continuity as children move from the Early Years Foundation Stage (DCSF, 2008) to Key Stage 1 of the National Curriculum (DfEE, 1999), as children move from a practical, play-based curriculum to a more structured activity-based curriculum in a way not necessarily conducive to smooth transition. Indeed the Rose review of primary education (Rose, 2009) recommends that Key Stage 1 builds upon the pedagogical successes of the Early Years Foundation Stage (DCSF, 2008), although it does not develop this idea fully in the context of mathematics (Thompson, 2009). There is a need for 'a coherent approach overall to the progression from EYFS to Year 1, and it is essential that the momentum in learning in mathematics is maintained through this transition' (Williams, 2008: 62).

Ways of using and exploring maths through games, applications and investigations can readily be extended throughout Key Stage 1 and generate rich opportunities for calculation. Games should ideally provide children with opportunities to make decisions and develop understanding as well as to practise simple calculations and recall of number bonds. In the best games everyone is calculating, even if only one player has the opportunity to make a move. For example, a simple board game such as snakes and ladders can be extended by using two dice and expecting the players to state whether they will add or subtract the numbers to determine their move. Adding the numbers means that you travel over more squares, but might just land you on a snake! Other players have an interest in knowing whether their opponent makes the best possible move, and are thus encouraged to calculate the possibilities even when it is not their turn to move.

A full class can be kept actively calculating with the game of Trice. The adult rolls three dice and records the three numbers. The class, working individually or in teams, have to use these digits to generate number sentences for as many of the numbers from 0 to 10 as they can. Almost every child will be able to add the numbers to give the total and to subtract one number from the other two. Some children will readily multiply and divide or use two numbers together to give a two digit number. As soon as there is any lapse in concentration, the adult rolls the dice to give three new numbers and the first set is removed. The winner is the first to generate all the required numbers. Although those with flexible calculating skills have an initial advantage, they too may be significantly challenged to generate the last few numbers: the game rewards skill, but requires luck. Another advantage of this very simple game is that it encourages children to use the symbols for operations which are much harder to grasp than the symbols for numbers (Hughes, 1986).

Applications of mathematics to include calculations can be both real and imaginary. Imaginary contexts can be developed from stories old or new. These provide a rich and compelling scenario in which children can pose and resolve problems, using calculation to aid the key characters. Particularly rich starting points are the many stories that involve conflicting worlds of different sizes. For example in *Jack and the Beanstalk* (Briggs, 1973): if the giant ate three boys

> The target is to generate the numbers 0–10
> The first roll of the dice gives 6, 3, 1
> $10 = 6 + 3 + 1$
> $9 = 6 + 3$
> 8
> $7 = 13 - 6$
> $6 = 6 \times 1$
> $5 = 6 - 1$
> $4 = 6 - 3 + 1$
> $3 = 6 - 3$
> $2 = 6 - 3 - 1$
> 1
> 0

Figure 2.2 The game of Trice

on toast, how big was his loaf of bread? Using the pictures, can we calculate how tall he would be? What could we use to give him a belt for his trousers? Whittaker (1986) describes a whole term of rich mathematical investigation, with slightly older children, based on the issue stated in the title *Will Gulliver's Suit Fit?*

Children of this age can also be encouraged to play an active role in using mathematics to plan and evaluate events. For example, how can we raise money at the school fair? What would be a fair price for the biscuits we are making? Can we organize a sports day where everyone is involved in exactly three events? Can we improve the dinner system so that we get more time to play? Such questions will lead to reasoning and calculations in real contexts and the answers may have a lasting impact on the way the school works.

Case study

One class of 7-year-olds decided to organize a healthy party feast. Instead of bringing food from home to share on the day, they researched appropriate recipes and each contributed some money towards the ingredients. They calculated the quantities of food they wanted and set out precise lists of the ingredients they needed. Looking again at the list, they tried to find ways of reducing the amount of food they would buy but not use. This set up new dilemmas to resolve: '*If we made the sweets smaller, do you think we could get 36 from just one packet of currants?*' '*It would be cheaper to add more cold tea and less lemonade, but would it taste nice?*' At last a small group was delegated to buy the ingredients which were then shared out to groups responsible for preparing different dishes. Some groups had to ensure that their mixture resulted in the right number of portions so that everyone would have a taste. There was much calculation and much fun. Lisa, visiting the school before transferring in the new term, was particularly thrilled. When her mother came to collect her she evaluated the day saying with glee: '*Oh I do want to come to this school because here we don't just have a party, we make a party happen!*'

Reflection for early career professional

- What calculations were involved in making the party happen?
- How could you help the children to use their mathematics during the planning?
- What opportunities are there in your class and school for extended mathematical applications?

Reflection for leader/manager

- How do you plan to develop the application of mathematics?
- Evaluate the risks and benefits of delegating organization of events to children of this age.

Investigations in maths require us to pose questions in an investigative style. Thus instead of asking closed questions such as *'What does seven and three make?'* or just writing '7 + 3 =, the adult (or child) can ask *'If 10 is the answer, what was the question?'* or *'What can we find out about the number 10?'* In one class exploring just this question Tim was happily listing subtractions 11–1, 12–2, 13–3 etc. to make ten and soon had a page full of calculations. Helen was less happy. She had chosen to add number pairs and had finally reduced her list to just 1 + 9, 2 + 8, 3 + 7, 4 + 6 and 5 + 5. What more could she do? Could Tim really have more answers than she had? Staring at the page she finally announced *'Perhaps there is something in between.'* She then tried 4 1/2 + 6 1/2, but realized this was too large and adjusted it to 4 1/2 + 5 1/2. At last she was happy again and was sure she could generate a lot more sums with ten as total. Of course, other children might have extended this work to include three numbers that added to ten, or to include zero and even negative numbers. But Helen's tactic was secure, reasoned and a real breakthrough in her thinking about number. She might pause here just using fractions of a half to extend her list, or she might begin to involve other fractions that she knew such as 1/4 or, using a calculator, move in to decimal notation. Her exploration is secure for as long as she can explain why her answer is correct.

The pedagogical demands of this change in moving to investigations in number should not be underestimated. The teacher loses the certainty of the order of presentation of maths topics in a text or framework and has to respond positively to new concepts when these are brought in to focus by the explorations of an individual or group. However, it is not enough to simply let this happen, the teacher needs to ensure that the new concepts are understood as an integral part of the number system. It is the children's certainty, or proof, that something is correct that is most important for the development of mathematics. For example, children will explore odd and even numbers. In many classes they will generate number pairs and notice the pattern that the sum of two odd numbers is an even number. However the fact that they have generated a few examples, should not in itself lead to the generalization that the sum of any two odd numbers is an even number. For this generalization to be justified the children will need to offer some level of proof. One such, from a 6-year-old, went like this. *'It's like when we go swimming and line up in pairs. If there are an odd number of children in our class, we can't do it properly, one person is left over. If there are an odd number of children next door they too will line up in pairs with one left over. But when we all go swimming together the left over children make another pair and the classes together are even!'* This is a naive visual proof of the generalization that two odd numbers make an even number. Although the expression is quirky and informal, it is a lot more powerful and mathematically impressive than simply showing that a number of pairs of specific odd numbers added together gave an even outcome.

This section has explored the following key aspects of calculating for 5–7-year-olds:

- Developing confidence in knowing and using number bonds strategically
- Using maths in increasingly complex applications through both imaginary and real scenarios
- Exploring the number system and developing a sense of certainty and proof.

Supporting the development of calculating

This final section of the chapter looks at how we can support young children as they develop their calculating skills and understandings. It is divided into three sections:

1. The early years environment, considering the adults who support learning and the environment in which the children learn.
2. Pedagogical approaches, which looks at the effectiveness of different approaches to calculating in the early years and provides some examples for reflection.
3. The leadership of mathematical development in the Early Years Foundation Stage.

The early years environment

Research from the EPPE (Effective Provision of Pre-School Education) project (Sylva et al., 2004) indicates the importance of the years before formal schooling in supporting children's development. There appear to be two key supporting factors: the quality of pre-school care and the role of parents and carers (Sylva et al., 2004). Williams (2008) refers directly to the EPPE research in acknowledgement of the cognitive benefits of effective early years education and care. Early years professionals need to be well qualified, to have good understanding of the effectiveness of different pedagogical approaches and to challenge children's thinking to develop reasoning skills – an essential element in effective calculating. The importance of parents and carers in understanding what early calculating is and supporting its development through quality interactions is another supportive factor for early years development (Walkerdine, 1988; Sylva et al., 2004; Williams, 2008).

The environments in which young children live and are cared for are rich with opportunities for calculating, but these are not always exploited to the full. Adults can seize and develop the opportunities that are there, challenging children to calculate and explore number, or they may be oblivious to these openings and let the opportunities pass by. Contrast two reception classes. In one, visiting students picked up on the excitement of some children approaching their fifth birthday and created an interactive display on the number five, only to be told that it should be removed forthwith because: *'We do not do five this term!'* In another reception class not far away, the teacher, Dom, uses every opportunity to explore number. At each registration the children count how many are absent and, with the support of a number line, create a number sentence to calculate how many are present; they share interesting numbers alongside interesting objects; they play number games with dice and cards; sing number songs as they tidy up and explore number patterns with calculators. Similarly you can contrast the use of the home environment to explore number. In one home, the use of number may be negligible or restricted to perhaps counting to five. In another, simple daily activities lead to opportunities to talk about maths while games with cards and dice support multiple calculations. Incidental calculations in the home might include: how many biscuits are needed for the whole family? How many more will be needed when visitors come? How long will it take for a favourite television programme to start? How much money should we take to the shops? Who is winning a game? How shall we plan a picnic? Why can't I have more sweets? Why do we pay the window cleaner? Where does money come from?

Photograph 2.3 Game to support calculation (© P. Hopkins)

There is evidence that the variation in the home maths experience of children is great (Tizard and Hughes, 1984; Walkerdine, 1988). Some parents and carers seize opportunities to engage in calculation spontaneously but more may be encouraged to take an active role in exploring situations mathematically. There is a role here for staff in early years settings and primary schools to be pro-active in sharing ideas and experiences. This could involve opportunities for parents and carers to experience activities in the setting (Mathematical Association, 1987); activities sent from the centre for families to work on together (Merttens and Vass, 1993) and specific paired work between child and adult (Topping and Bamford, 1998). Key features of all these approaches are that the activities should be enjoyable and extendable offering both repetitive practice and genuine challenge.

Practical tasks

Are there ways in which your setting could support the development of mathematical language and problem solving at home?

- Organize a family maths trail inside and outside the setting.
- Collect number songs and rhymes and include one in each newsletter.
- If there is a community literacy group, consider whether there is a need for a family maths group which could include activities for carers and children together.
- Develop game packs to go home on loan for a week including everything needed for a game of number snap etc.
- Send home a mathematical problem or challenge for children to tackle with family and friends for example, '*How many things can you fit into a yoghurt pot?*' or '*Can you show 100?*' and display the results in the reception area for everyone to see and talk about.
- Include calculating activities in story sacks and encourage carers to use these alongside the story itself.
- Run curriculum events where children engage adults in number games and activities.
- Invite parents to share their skills of cooking, craft work etc. with children in the setting and work with them to make the opportunities for mathematics and calculating explicit.

When you have tried out some of these ideas evaluate the success of them.

Reflection for early career professional

- How could you promote calculating opportunities in the home for the children in your class?
- What are the challenges/ obstacles to overcome in this promotion?
- How can you overcome these challenges?

Reflection for leader/manager

- How could you further opportunities for calculating in the home through whole school/setting initiatives?
- What are the main factors supporting and hindering improved home/setting calculating experiences?
- How can you overcome the obstacles you have identified?

Pedagogical approaches

Practical play approaches are recognized through early childhood theories (Froebel, 1826; Piaget, 1950; Bruner, 1960; Vygotsky, 1978), through national strategies from Plowden (DES, 1967) to the Early Years Foundation Stage (DCSF, 2008) and are also advocated in early years literature (Bennett, et al., 1997; Johnston, 2002; BERA, 2003; Moyles, 2005). Gopnik in *The Philosophical Baby* reaffirms and further develops the importance of play in children's lives: *'Play is the signature of childhood. It's a living, visible manifestation of imagination and learning in action. It's also the most visible sign of the paradoxically useful uselessness of immaturity. By definition, play – the baby nesting blocks and pushing the buttons of a busy box, the toddler pretending to be everything from a mermaid to a ninja – has no obvious point or goal or function . . . And yet these useless actions . . . are distinctively, characteristically human and deeply valuable'* (Gopnik, 2009: 14).

In nurseries, play groups and other early years settings, the opportunities for play can include absorbing role-play areas, planned carefully to ensure opportunities for the development of calculation skills. Hughes et al. (2000) advocate planning activities for young children that involve application of calculating skills and understandings. In many play activities children will be able to see the relevance of calculating to everyday life and begin to apply their skills and understandings. For example in a post office play area, children can sort the mail alphabetically, calculate how many letters are in the pile for names beginning with A, how many more/less in the pile beginning with S, how many letter there are all together, who has the most/least letters etc. Other calculating experiences can come from using and handling the money in the post office, sorting different stamps, envelopes and parcels. Professionals should also recognize and use the outdoor environment as a rich environment for development: including age old games like hopscotch or skipping and long-term project activities such as establishing and caring for a garden area etc.

Case study

In the Reception class, the role-play area was set up as a seaside, with sand on the floor and a collection of shells, plastic crabs and sand worms in the sand and a water trough with a collection of plastic fish of different sizes and colours and types. While five 4-year-old children were playing in the role-play area, they dug up the shells with small spades and put them into buckets. Sonia said to Ricki, *'My bucket is bigger than yours'* and Ricki disagreed, asking the teaching assistant to agree with him. She asked the children how they could find out which bucket was the biggest and Sonia said *'Mine has more shells'* and Louis said *'Count them'*. The TA thought this was a good idea and so the children began to count how many shells were in each bucket. When they had finished they had counted one very large shell and six small shells in Sonia's bucket and *'hundreds of small shells'* in Ricki's bucket, which when counted out were really 43. Sonia said *'that's not fair, mine's bigger'* and so the TA asked how the children could calculate how big the buckets were fairly. Louis said that they should use all small shells, but Sonia and Ricki felt that big ones would be better as they were easier to count. Once they had decided this, the TA was able to leave them to calculate how many big shells they could fit in the buckets. Later she suggested to them that they could also make a sandcastle and see which was the biggest and Louis decided to make sandcastles using each of the five plastic buckets in the sand. His first attempt was not very good as the dry sand just made a pile and Paulo suggested that he used some water to make the sand wet. This was much more successful and Paulo helped Louis to make the castle and decide which bucket was biggest.

Dipa and Frankie were playing with the 'fish' in the water trough and the teacher asked them if they could fish out three blue fish. Dipa asked *'Do you want big or small ones?'*. The teachers asked for three small blue long fish and Dipa fished them out. *'Do you want some more?'* said Frankie and the teacher said *'Yes please. Can I have five big red fish and one small yellow fish please?'* Frankie fished them out and laid them on the table. *'How many fish have you fished out altogether?'* said the teacher. The children counted out the 3 fish that Dipa had 'caught' and the five plus one fish that Frankie had fished out. *'I have three said Dipa and you have six.'* *'How many is that altogether?'* said the teacher and they all counted the fish together. *'Nine, nine',* they both said.

Reflection for early career professional

There are opportunities for calculating all around us, in the indoor and outdoor classroom and in role play and exploratory activities and games.

- What opportunities are there in your classroom at the moment for calculating?
- How could you extend the opportunities for calculating in your classroom?
- How can you best interact with the children in your class to encourage and extend calculating?

Case study—Cont'd

Reflection for leader/manager

Consider your current role-play areas.

- Do they provide opportunities for calculating?
- How do you currently support development in calculating?
- How could you improve both the opportunities and support for calculating?

Photograph 2.4 Opportunities for calculating (© P. Hopkins)

Pedagogical support initiatives for low achievers, such as Mathematics Recovery (Wright et al., 2006) and Every Child Counts (Edge Hill University, 2009) are based on practical and supported activities which aim to improve the rate of mathematical development. Mathematics Recovery employs a constructivist approach, starting with interviews to elicit children's current mathematical understanding and using enquiry-based activities with ample time for children to solve genuine problems and supported by knowledgeable adults. One very good rationale for this approach is that children are motivated to engage in the calculations, and this aides their development. The Every Child Counts programme targets children who by Year 2 have fallen behind in mathematics and involves training teachers who make daily one-to-one and small group interventions. Initial results (Edge Hill University, 2009) show the children involved progressed at four times the expected rate. While Every Child Counts is designed as an intervention programme for children at the end of Key Stage 1, it, together with the Mathematics Recovery initiative, raises questions about developing pedagogical approaches for younger children that could prevent the necessity of intervention. Would practical, short, individually tailored enquiry that supports children in developing their skills and understandings of calculation in intriguing contexts lead to more secure and established understanding of all?

Early years professionals should attempt to show children that calculating occurs in a great many everyday contexts and give children the time needed to explore, practise and extend their calculating skills (DCSF, 2008), seeking patterns, making connections and recognizing relationships in their calculations. It is easy in a very busy curriculum to rush from one activity to another, in order to ensure coverage. However, without the time to think, reflect and reason, children will not make the developments we would like and expect.

Professionals should also consciously develop and use mathematical vocabulary during play, practical activities and daily routines (DCSF, 2008). For example, when doing the register, children can count the number of children present, calculate those absent or how many more boys there are than girls. At snack times they can calculate how many glasses/cartons of milk are needed, how many children want apple, banana or orange to eat and what is the favourite choice of fruit.

Reflection for early career professional

- How important do you think mathematical talk is?
- How do you currently promote mathematical talk in your classroom?

Reflection for leader/manager

- Audit the actual talk that happens during different activities: Who talks? Who listens? Who answers?

Reflection—Cont'd

- Are there ways in which your setting could extend the development of mathematical talk between children?

Practical tasks

- Record the discussions when children play at maths games or in the role-play area
- Record the discussions when adults take part in the play
- How can you further prompt children to talk about their calculation strategies and why they know an answer is right?

Leading development in calculating

Some research studies (Jefferies et al., 2003) have linked low birth weight and a poor childhood socio-economic environment with ongoing cognitive difficulties in maths (as well as reading). The difficulties observed have been seen to persist even in late teens and early adulthood and this has raised concerns about very premature children being treated in the same way as other children with regards to starting school. Other researchers (e.g. Cockcroft, 1982; Hughes, 1986; Wright, 1994; Aubrey, 1997) have noted the wide range of abilities displayed by young children. Wright (1994) suggests that 5-year-olds entering school had diverse number knowledge with some displaying only that of a typical 2-year-old and others that of an 8-year-old. This attainment gap often seems to widen, rather than narrow, through schooling and the problem may be further exacerbated if low attainers develop a negative attitude to maths activities (Wright, 1994).

Such findings have implications for our support of the children in our care. There is a need to take account of each child's starting point and to provide differentiation both through varied starting points, degrees of challenge and access to support. Sometimes this can be achieved through a single open-ended activity. For example, Lisa and Kali were using the constant addition function of a calculator to display numbers in sequence. Although seven years of age, they had not fully understood the patterns of counting numbers beyond about 30. To them the calculator provided fascinating reinforcement of the changing digits in units, tens and hundreds. Meanwhile Jeremy and Rebecca watched them at work and pondered: *'How long would it take to reach a million?' 'I wonder what is the biggest number you could display?'* etc. They were thus able to set themselves appropriate challenges from the same starting activity. At other times different groups and individuals will need distinct activities to provide the right level of challenge. Thus, for example, in a role-play area the shopkeeper requires greater confidence in calculating than the shopper. The shopper can select items and proffer some money, whereas the shopkeeper has to provide a reasonable total for the purchases, accept the money as sufficient and calculate the correct change.

The challenges for the leader in developing an environment that fosters calculation are thus to provide a richly mathematical environment, to ensure that adults support children's exploration of the mathematical activities and to provide genuine mathematical challenge for both low attainers and the mathematically gifted.

Photograph 2.5 Calculating in an early years setting (photograph by Emma Jordan)

Practical tasks

Here is an activity to try with your staff to instigate fierce discussion about mathematics explorations. Each person should place three paper cups upright on the table. A *move* is to turn any two cups the other way up. By using moves, can you rearrange the cups so that all three are upside down?

Try this activity yourself now.

In fact this task is impossible. It will make some colleagues angry that you even asked them to try it. But with some prompting you can help them to see that moving from *'I can't do this'* to *'This can't be done'* is empowering. You can extend this investigation by exploring when the task is possible or impossible using different numbers of cups and different 'moves'.

Reflections

- What opportunities do we provide for children to tussle with problems mathematically?
- Do we provide circumstances and time to encourage children to state why their answer is correct, or incorrect?
- Are there activities which leave the most able struggling to succeed and the least able confident in their answers, as well as the other way round?

Further reflection for early career professional

- Put yourself in the position of a child in your class and consider how some of the tasks you set them make them feel?
- How can you help children to feel positive and excited about exploring and calculating?

Further reflection for leader/manager

- How could you promote a culture where children feel secure enough to take risks in their calculating and where they feel challenged, but not frustrated?

Conclusion

In this chapter we have aimed to show that a range of simple activities in homes, early years settings and classrooms can be explored and exploited to give children opportunities to develop their calculating skills and their confidence in working mathematically. Subtle shifts in the way activities are presented and responded to can significantly enrich the environment for calculating and should increase the mathematical confidence and understanding of young learners.

References

Atkinson, S. (ed.) (1992), *Mathematics with Reason: The Emergent Approach to Primary Maths.* London: Hodder and Stoughton

Aubrey, C. (1997), 'Children's early learning of number in school and out' Chapter 2 in Thompson, I. (ed.) *Teaching and Learning Early Number.* Buckingham: Open University Press, pp. 20–29

BBC (2006), '*How Babies do Maths at 7 Months*'. BBC News http://news.bbc.co.uk/2/hi/science/nature/4713714.stm accessed 3/4/09

BBC (2009), *Horizon 'Who Do You Want Your Child to Be' BBC Two, 16 March 2009.* London: BBC

Bennett N, Wood L and Rodgers S (1997), *Teaching Through Play: Teachers Thinking and Classroom Practice.* Buckingham: Open University Press

BERA Early Years Special Interest Group (2003), *Early Years Research: Pedagogy, Curriculum and Adult Roles, Training and Professionalism.* Southwell, Notts: BERA

Bird, M. H. (1991), *Mathematics for Young Children: An Active Thinking Approach.* London: Routledge

Briggs, R. (1973), *Jim and the Beanstalk.* London: Penguin

Bruner, J. (1960), *The Process of Education.* Harvard: Harvard University Press

Cockcroft, W. H. (1982), *Mathematics Counts: Report to the Committee of Inquiry onto Teaching of Mathematics in Schools.* London: HMSO

Compton A. K. J. (2010), 'Numbers as labels and for counting' in Johnston J. (ed.) *Problem Solving, Reasoning and Numeracy.* London: Continuum

DCSF (2008), *The Early Years Foundation Stage; Setting the Standard for Learning, Development and Care for Children from Birth to Five; Practice Guidance.* London: DCSF

DES (1967), *Children and their Primary School: A Report of the Central Advisory Council for Education (England) Vol. 1: Report.* London: HMSO

de Bóo M (2004), *The Curriculum Partnership: Early Years Handbook.* Sheffield: Geography Association

DfEE (1999a), *The National Curriculum. Handbook for Primary Teachers in England.* London: QCA

DfEE (1999b), *The National Numeracy Strategy.* London: DFEE

DfES (2006), *Primary Framework for Literacy and Mathematics.* London: DfES

Edge Hill University (2009), *Numbers Count.* Ormskirk: Edge Hill University

Ensing, J. and Spencer, B. (2003), *Children Learning: Mathematical Development: A Handbook to Support Good Practice for the Early Years.* Walton on Thames: Spencer Publications

Froebel, F. (1826), *On the Education of Man.* Keilhau, Leipzig: Wienbrach

Gifford, S (2005), *Teaching Mathematics 3–5: Developing Learning in the Foundation Stage.* Maidenhead: Open University Press

Gopnik, A. (2009), *The Philosophical Baby: What Children's Minds Tell Us about Truth, Love and the Meaning of Life.* London: Bodley Head

Griffiths, R. (1988), *Maths through Play. Easy Paths to Early Learning with your Child.* London: Macdonald and Co.

Hall, N (1989), *Writing with Reason.* London: Hodder and Stoughton

Haylock, D. and Cockburn, A. (2003), *Understanding Mathematics in the Lower Primary Years: a Guide for Teachers of Children 3–8 2nd Edition.* London: Paul Chapman

Hughes, M. (1986), *Children and Number: Difficulties in Learning Mathematics.* Oxford: Basil Blackwell

Hughes, M., Desforges, C and Mitchell, C. with Carré, C. (2000), *Numeracy and Beyond: Applying Mathematics in the Primary School.* Buckingham: Open University Press

Jordan, K. E. and Brannon, E. M. (2006), 'The multisensory representation of number in infancy' *Proceedings of the National Academy of Sciences of the United States of America.* 28 February 2006. vol. 103. no. 9 pp.3486–3489

Johnson, A., Bowler, U., Yudkin, P., Hockley, C., Wariyar, U., Gardner, F. and Mutch, L. (2003), 'Health and school performance of teenagers born before 29 weeks gestation'. *Arch. Dis. Child. Fetal Neonatal Ed.,* May 2003; 88: F190 F198

Johnston, J. (2002), 'Teaching and learning in the early years' in Johnston, J., Chater, M. and Bell, D. (ed.) *Teaching the Primary Curriculum.* Buckingham: Open University Press, 24–37

Johnston, J. and Nahmad-Williams, L. (2008), *Early Childhood Studies.* Harlow: Pearsons

Kamii, C. K. (1989), *Young Children Continue to Re-invent Arithmetic Second Grade: Implications of Piaget's Theory.* New York: Teachers' College Press

Mathematical Association (1987), *Sharing Mathematics with Parents.* Cheltenham: Stanley Thornes

Merttens, R. and Vass, J. (eds) (1993), *Partnership in Maths: Parents and Schools.* London: Falmer Press

Moyles, J. (2005), *The Excellence of Play 2nd Edition.* Maidenhead: Open University Press

Nunes, T. and Bryant, P. (1996), *Children Doing Mathematics.* Oxford: Blackwell

Piaget, J. (1950), *The Psychology of Intelligence.* London: Routledge and Kegan Paul

Pound, L. (2006), *Supporting Mathematical Development in the Early Years.* Second Edition. Maidenhead: Open University Press

Primary National Strategy, (2006), *Seamless Transitions – Supporting Continuity in Young Children's Learning* Norwich: Sure Start/ DfES

Rose, J. (2009), *Independent Review of the Primary Curriculum: Final Report.* Nottingham: DCFS

Sanders, D., White, G., Burge, B., Sharp, C., Eames, A., McEune, R and Grayson, NFER, H. (2005), *A Study of the Transition from the Foundation Stage to Key Stage 1.* London: Surestart

Scottish Consultative Council on the Curriculum (2003), *Numeracy in the Early Years. What Research Tells Us* 4th Edition. Glasgow: Learning and Teaching Scotland

Shuard, H., Walsh, A., Goodwin, J. and Worcester, V. (1991), *Calculators, Children and Mathematics.* London: Simon and Schuster

Sylva, K., Melhuish, E., Sammons, P., Siraj-Blatchford, I.and Taggart, B. (2004), *The Effective Provision of Pre-School Education (Eppe) Project: Final Report – A Longitudinal Study Funded by The DfES 1997–2004.* London: DfES

Thompson, I. (2009), 'Place Value?' *Mathematics Teaching* 215, 4–5 September 2009

Topping, K. and Bamford, J. (1998), *Parental Involvement and Peer Tutoring in Maths and Science.* London: Fulton

Tizard, B. and Hughes, M. (1984), *Young Children Learning.* London: Fontana

Trundley, R. (2008), 'The Value of Two' *Mathematics Teaching* 211, (November), 17–19

Vygotsky, L., Cole, M. (ed.), (1978), *Mind in Society: the Development of Higher Psychological Processes.* Cambridge, MA: Harvard University Press

Walkerdine, V. (1988), *The Mastery of Reason.* London: Routledge

Whittaker, D. E. (1986), *Will Gulliver's Suit Fit? Mathematical Problem-Solving with Children.* Cambridge: CUP

Williams, P. (2008), *Independent Review of Mathematics Teaching in Early Years Settings and Primary Schools.* London: DCSF

Worthington, M. and Carruthers, E. (2003), *Children's Mathematics: Making Marks, Making Meaning.* London: Paul Chapman

Wright, R. J. (1994), 'A study of the numerical development of 5-year-olds and 6-year-olds' *Educational Studies in Mathematics,* 26, 25–44

Wright, R. J., Martland, J. and Stafford, A. K. (2006), *Early Numeracy: Assessment for Teaching and Intervention.* London: Paul Chapman

3 Shape, Space and Measures

Introduction

The Early Years Foundation Stage framework covering the area of learning Problem Solving, Reasoning and Numeracy states shape, space and measures *'is about how, through talking about shapes and quantities, and developing appropriate vocabulary, children use their knowledge to develop ideas and to solve mathematical problems'*. This chapter provides a focus on shape, space and measures, covering activities young children might experience in their active play and learning during the early years from birth to eight and the theory and rationale underpinning the area of learning. This will be discussed in phases birth to three, three to five and five to seven, although awareness of progression at different times appropriate to children as individuals, is recognized. The area of learning based on this aspect is considered as part of an holistic approach to learning and development. The crucial nature of the adult interactions of those who are involved with the young children's learning is incorporated, with research evidence and differing theoretical stances underpinning the deliberations. The role of the leader of the various settings is discussed in terms of working in a team to organize, manage and promote the best possible experiences and environment for the children in their care. Practical examples and case studies are described.

Shape, space and measures

Hopkins et al. (1999: 72) emphasize the importance of shape and space as part of the curriculum stating *'valuing the space and shape curriculum is an important start to develop children's spatial mathematical ability'*. It promotes an understanding of the 3-D world in which the children live. Carruthers et al. (2006: xvii) note that this is achieved while there is *'a move away from a subject based curriculum'* to the recognition that each subject is *'intertwined and therefore interdependent'*.

Case study

As part of activities following interest in the arrival of a local fair, children constructed fair ground rides using articles brought from home and equipment available in the setting. This successfully linked with other areas of learning, for example designing and planning routes and pathways for the rides and stalls, accounts of visits to the fair, role play of a fairground ride, selling tickets and using the roles at the fair, baking biscuits for the stalls, painting posters and organizing the outdoor area as our own fairground. Children practised their skills throwing 3-D soft shapes into buckets, hopscotch and made equipment for games.

Reflection for early career professional

- What activities are available based on shape, space and measures, for the children to access independently?
- Can awareness of this aspect of learning be incorporated into other areas of the Early Years Foundation Stage framework activities developed?

Case study—Cont'd

Reflection for leader/manager

- How is awareness of shape, space and measures promoted throughout the learning environment?
- How are resources organized to facilitate ease of learning?
- Who has responsibility for the area of learning?
- Are the resources appropriate for adult-led and independent activities?

Shape and space

According to Haylock et al. (1989: 95) in mathematics number is '*essentially an activity that involves the left hemisphere of the brain*' whereas '*spatial thinking functions through the right hemisphere.*' Consideration is given to children's prior knowledge regarding the area of learning, liaison with parents/carers to broaden the understanding of those responsible for their care, different teaching and learning styles can impact on individual progress, with planning needed to ensure inclusive practice. Clemson et al. (1994: 19) argue that in schools '*a wide range of mathematical ideas should be available to children, and in a variety of classroom created contexts.*'

Measures

The activities described for young children develop from non-standard measures to the introduction of standard measurements. Nearly all measurement is approximate and attempts to give an accurate recording with the equipment available. Volume measures the amount of 3-D space occupied, while capacity concerns the containers that identify the volume of liquid held. Through play children can discover the properties of shape, space and measures, for example discovering that water is displaced when playing in the water trough. Archimedes found the volume of a hand by placing it in a container full of water and measuring the amount of water that was displaced. The water that was displaced was poured into a measuring jug.

Research

Fuyset al. (1988) highlight the importance of introducing children to the properties of shapes and special awareness from an early age, to provide a foundation of knowledge and understanding about shapes and space for later learning.

Battista (1999) emphasizes the notion of *'spatial structuring'* which concerns internalizing the mental processes of special awareness. This is deemed to be relevant for gaining an understanding of spatial perspectives while significantly supporting the child's awareness of their place in their surroundings.

The Williams Report

The Williams Report (2008: 32) identifies clear guidelines for the ways forward for provision for mathematics in the early years. It states *'Central to effective mathematical pedagogy in the early years is fostering children's natural interest in numeracy, problem solving, reasoning, shapes and measures.'* The report emphasizes the importance of children's mathematical mark making. This can be encouraged by having suitable materials available in all areas to aid the ease of use, provide a reminder to record thoughts, ideas and designs, reinforce the importance placed on mark making, encourage shared discussions of plans, support visualization of properties, while celebrating and valuing children's views.

Those responsible for children's learning and development are also mentioned. Adults working with young children should have a *'clear grasp of how children's understanding of mathematical concepts such as shape, space, measure, numbers and problem solving develops, and appropriate ways of developing a learning environment that facilitates learning about these things through play'* (Williams, 2008: 40).

Historical aspects

Mathematical applications have their origins in the practical use needed to construct such structures as pyramids and stone circles. Cooke (2000: 98) notes that although the area of learning is often called shape and space, *'geometry is the original term for the study of relationships between points, lines, circles, planes and other 2-D and 3-D shapes.'* It could have arisen from the use as a practical measurement of land in the Nile Delta in Ancient Egypt and developed by the Greeks around 500 BC. The Greek civilization contributed through developing understanding about mathematics, for example the theories of Pythagoras, Eulid, Eratosthenes and Archimedes. Early Greek mathematics drew much of its work from the Babylonians and Egyptians but developed the work as an abstract subject. Clemson et al. (1994: 43) argue *'many of us will be familiar with the notion of theorems in which logically argued proofs are used to establish things like the shortest distance between two points and the sum of the angles of a triangle.'*

The earliest recorded units of length were based on body parts, for example use of the span – measurement from the tip of the thumb to the tip of the little finger on an extended hand or the cubit which measures the forearm from the elbow to the tip of the middle finger. The measures are readily available and easily moved to the desired locations. The Romans refined systems of measurement, with the use of hands and feet as part of the applied systems. The human body could be readily used for shared measurements. In communities, common understandings of measures could flourish. However, as people travelled further afield there was a need for more standard measurements to aid fair exchanges and collaboration. Electricity and new forms of technology supported the development of refined electronic measurements which could more accurately provide measurements for length, mass and time. Technologies and new software appropriate for children based on shape, space and measures can be used by those working with young children to support the developing awareness of the area of learning. *'We can harness new technologies in getting children to expand their vision of what is possible in mathematics'* (Clemson et al., 1994: 55).

Care can be taken to ensure that correct vocabulary is used in sessions, such as the use of the term polyhedra, which are a group of solids that have all their faces made of flat surfaces, for example a cube is a polyhedra while a cylinder is not. Mooney et al. (2007: 145) suggest that *'misconceptions can easily develop, with children confusing concepts and using them as if they were interchangeable.'* For example volume is the 3-D space that is occupied, measured in cubic units. Capacity describes how much liquid volume a container holds.

Shapes in the surroundings can be observed in 'shape walks' and games used to help children become aware of natural shapes around them. This can foster children's awareness of shapes used indoors which do not commonly exist naturally. Ancient Egyptians used a plumb bob and shadow stick to measure the length of the shadow cast by the sun. This demonstrated an appreciation of imaginary lines to create a triangle and led to the use of the shape as a right-angled triangle in constructions and measurements. When children are using shapes in play they can become aware of the properties of the shapes and how they can be utilized in a broad sense.

Patterns can be discussed to appreciate different forms, such as symmetrical, reflective and rotational. Patterns can be observed in number, for example in triangular numbers or square numbers.

Shape, space and measures from birth to 3 years of age

Hopkins et al. (1999: 72) identify that work on shape, space and measures 'can sometimes lack a sense of purpose and progression'. Activities relating to problem solving are particularly emphasized, which includes reasoning, communicating and visualizing. Children's active involvement with activities provide investigations, exploration and consolidation of knowledge and understanding about properties of shape, awareness of space and measures which can be scaffolded through interactions with others. This supports the growing awareness of properties and aids children's abilities to visualize them.

Shape, space and measures form part of the Early Years Foundation Stage (EYFS) Learning and Development framework in the Problem Solving, Reasoning and Numeracy area. The discussion of children's progress is in three parts; numbers for labels and for counting, calculating and shape, space and measures. The EYFS (DCSF, 2008: 63) framework states that *'Children must be supported in developing their understanding of Problem Solving, Reasoning and Numeracy in a broad range of contexts in which they can explore, enjoy, learn, practise and talk about their developing understanding. They must be provided with opportunities to practise these skills and to gain confidence and competence in their use.'* The framework is underpinned by consideration of the child as a unique individual, forming positive relationships within enabling environments. The EYFS states 'Babies' and children's mathematical development occurs as they seek patterns, make connections and recognize relationships through finding out about and working with numbers and counting, with sorting and matching and with shape, space and measures.' The developmental framework starts at children's birth and is in stages consisting of birth–11 months, 8–20 months, 16–26 months, 22–36 months, 30–50 months and 40–60 + months. The age phases overlap to illustrate the individuality of children's development throughout the stages. The vocabulary used in the framework identifies the emphasis placed on the process of the learning to develop understanding. The format of the framework enables providers to observe, assess and build on previous learning to ensure children can progress and develop.

Concepts can be formed and consolidated throughout children's everyday lives. '*Children use their knowledge and skills in these areas to solve problems, generate new questions and make connections across other areas of Learning and Development*' (EYFS, 2008). Shape, space and measures aspects will be incorporated not only within other Problem Solving, Reasoning and Numeracy areas but as part of the wider areas of learning, including Personal, Social and Emotional, Communication Language and Literacy, Knowledge and Understanding of the World, Physical Development and Creative Development. Children can access activities at an appropriate level for their development in both limited age and mixed aged groups frequently found in early years provision.

Very young children's exploration of their surroundings can promote awareness of shapes, space and measures. Play with 3-D shapes encourages understanding of how the different shapes move, how they move and the ease or difficulty that arises when various shapes are incorporated into play. Knowledge of the properties of shapes, spatial awareness and measures can be consolidated through the exploration of resources and the environment to promote investigations. Children can learn to handle and observe the effects of movements of shapes and how they can be perceived from different viewpoints. Edwards (1998: 156) claims '*there is no substitute for exploring and comparing real objects.*' She continues, '*Pictures on paper cannot provide the visual or spatial experiences required for children to understand fully the properties of shapes.*' Children can demonstrate a variety of approaches to play, for example epistemic play behaviours concern the acquisition of knowledge and skills, while ludic play behaviour consolidates learning and practises mathematical skills previously gained.

Case study

A 3-year-old observed grass and leaves falling down a slide. A children's ball rolled down the slide. The child then attempted to use the slide. She picked up the ball and experimented rolling the ball purposefully along the floor.

Giving young children the opportunity to investigate shapes helps to develop their thinking skills, build concepts through concrete experiences, enhance understanding and vocabulary through discussions with others and fosters further enquiry about their world. Very young children use their senses to further explore objects and materials around them. Interactions with others can promote young children's social communication and knowledge and understanding of the world, for example discussion with adults during journeys, particularly familiar ones, can support children's understanding of space. Routine activities can be incorporated into this growing awareness of the area of learning, for example getting dressed, size of clothes or their own level of growth.

Reflections for early career professionals

- Are children able to gain access to a variety of sensory resources in their play?
- How can these be used to promote awareness of the aspect of learning?

Reflections for leader/manager

- How is this area of learning included into planning to enable other adults in the setting to be aware of the possibilities?
- Are children's ideas developed to encourage their construction of concepts and ideas?
- Are the outdoor and indoor environment fully utilized to incorporate learning for shape, space and measures?

Very young children can be involved with their learning from the earliest days. Eye contact with familiar adults and use of activities involving sensory awareness promote children's safe and happy development, for example talk and response with the child or play with balls, boxes or such items as shaped biscuits. Nutbrown and Page (2008: 154) cite Goldschmied's work promoting children's heuristic play with objects. This consists of offering a group of children a large number of different kinds of objects and receptacles with which they play freely without adult intervention.

Very young children thrive on a happy, safe environment provided for them. Within this environment knowledge and understanding of shapes, space and measures can be enhanced through a developing awareness in everyday procedures, such as dressing, setting the table or playing with toys, while creative opportunities can be seized led by the child, to gain further understanding, for example an observation of the shape of a wheel. Children can be encouraged to think of responses and possible reasons for themselves, with adult interaction to stimulate their thinking. Appropriate questioning can encourage children's interests from closed questions, such as what is it, to more open questions, for example could the shapes fit together.

Shape, space and measures from 3 to 5 years of age

Shapes can be introduced through discussions of items, such as a favourite toy to describe basic properties of the shape. Children can be encouraged to notice shapes in the environment including door handles, windows or bricks. Play equipment, for example balls, cylinders and large construction equipment can be used as a resource as an ongoing reminder of the identification of properties of shapes. 3-D materials can be used as part of creative development to consolidate learning and provide a range of learning styles for children. Games, shape pictures and barrier games can be accessed as the children play. Appropriate mark making tools should be provided to allow children to experiment with the resources. Construction equipment and a variety of materials can be organized to support children's independent learning in the environment of the setting. Activities can be devised to collaborate with parents or carers, for example houses made with identification of shapes used. The model houses can then be used to design a model area of the town, village or street in the city to support children's awareness of where they live and the community around them. Positional language can be enhanced through everyday activities and structured ones, for example setting a table, while organizing and playing with toys or negotiating places for objects in a game.

According to Pound (2003: 38) *'The measurement of length, mass, volume, capacity and even time is part of many day-to-day conversations.'* Recipes are an enjoyable way to develop and consolidate knowledge and understanding in all areas of the framework. Children can devise their own recipes, for example making sandwiches and follow made recipes. These can be written to enable young children to follow the instructions, such as washing hands. Ingredients could be measured using cups or spoons to enhance children's ability to access the recipes. A visit to the shops provides an understanding of exchanging money and how food is sorted. In a role-play area table cutlery can be organized by colour sorting items and shapes to match. Three-dimensional shapes can be made from construction equipment or own made to support learning. Resources and materials could be accessible to make articles such as a Toy Box for the setting, homes, dens, shops, garages and smaller items, for example a container for a gift.

Children are fascinated by symmetrical patterns which can be introduced at an early age through practical activities such as painting symmetrical wings for a butterfly model. Children enjoy making their own patterns, which can be displayed to support discussions and help children attempt different ones. Patterns can be displayed around the setting to reinforce the concept, such as the use of soles of boots printed to identify an alternate differently coloured pattern, or any relevant object to link with a medium term theme, for example prints of circles when thinking about wheels.

Case study

Children were introduced to pattern by discussing patterns on paper and made patterns using early years equipment. These were introduced throughout the setting using such activities as eggmen patterns repeating those already completed, developing the difficulty of patterns from repeated patterns in twos to three, four or more. Large construction bricks were patterned when building walls for houses made following a visit to a nearby Show house, printed patterns were painted for the wallpaper of a large house that had been constructed, Diwali patterns were discussed and painted, patterns in the indoor and outdoor environment were observed.

Case study—Cont'd

Reflections for early career professionals

- How can awareness of pattern be incorporated into activities and displays?
- Can children be encouraged to make their own patterns to use in their play?

Reflections for leader/manager

- How can awareness of pattern be included into other aspects of learning, for example when promoting a diverse ethos and awareness of pattern in the environment both made and natural?

Awareness of space can be developed through discussions based on children's experiences for example of the locality of areas within the setting.

Formative assessments should be maintained throughout the child's attendance at the setting with collaboration with colleagues and parents/carers. They follow the framework in the six broad areas of development culminating in the Early Learning Goals. These consist of:

- Using language such as 'greater', 'smaller', 'heavier' or 'lighter' to compare quantities
- Talking about, recognizing and recreating simple patterns
- Using language such as 'circle' or 'bigger' to describe the shape and size of solids and flat shapes

Children will be summatively assessed at the end of the reception year as part of the Early Years Foundation Stage Profile.

The EYFS builds progression from birth to age five and therefore reinforces the seamless development and consolidation of learning through the ages phases as children grow. Children are able to explore through their senses and using equipment and facilities available to them. Small groups of young children can devise experiments and investigations to enhance their understanding of the area of learning, for example building using manufactured shapes, designing and making containers for such things as fruit or presents for a loved one. When young children are involved in their learning and understand the context and purpose of the investigations, activities became exciting and enthralling.

Case study

A group of four, 4-year-olds decided to make a bridge using the wooden blocks available. Much discussion, planning and designing took place before the bridge was built. When it was built further deliberations resulted in changes to the design following discussions of strength of the bridge (could it carry the required vehicles and loads), suitability for the space and consideration of elements it spanned. Children's problems in play can be used as a tool for learning about shapes, space and measures, for example large buildings made as part of the story 'Little Red Riding Hood' could be incorporated for the shape of the parts of the buildings or length of path needed between the houses.

Reflections for early career professionals

- How can appropriate mathematical language be used in children's play?
- In what ways can children be helped to scaffold their learning, building on their existing knowledge and understanding?

Reflections for leader/manager

- Are opportunities provided in the setting for children to work independently, in small and large groups to support their learning?
- Are a range of learning opportunities encouraged, for example the use of talk to enable children to share their knowledge and ideas?

Transition to Key Stage 1 (5 to 7 years of age)

A smooth transition from experiences during birth–5 provision leads into Key Stage 1 where activities are planned based on the Early Years Foundation Stage to the Primary Numeracy Strategy. Activities should draw on children's knowledge and understanding and provide stimulating and fun experiences, focusing on active, meaningful learning. Standard measures can be introduced to develop from those based on non-standard items. The National programmes of Study clearly state the knowledge, skills and understanding which are to be taught in Key Stage 1. This provides a seamless transition form the Early Years Foundation Stage. Children need to be increasingly able to describe the properties of 2-D and 3-D shapes, to support their visualization of activities and aid problem-solving capabilities. A variety of symmetrical patterns can be introduced and a growing awareness of space fostered. Appropriate vocabulary can be used to support children's special awareness and understanding of measures. Comparisons and uniform non-standard measures can be used with the introduction of standard measures such as metres and litres and later centimetres and kilograms. Children from an early age choose the equipment they would like to use in their play. As they become more proficient with the resources available they are increasingly able to choose appropriately for the required task, become more confident with measurement and the use of tools to achieve it. Progress throughout children's learning should be assessed and observed to ensure that further progress and consolidation and enthusiasm are maintained and encouraged and activities are appropriate for the child.

Case study

Children enjoy exploring 3-D equipment to design their own constructions. This approach was used as an ongoing facility in a Key Stage 1 classroom where children were encouraged to create their own designs, discover properties of their constructions and share them in a specially devised display, to the rest of the class.

Activities based on shape, space and measures can continue to be promoted through children's interests, in meaningful contexts and through their involvement in the tasks devised. Excitement for the area of learning can be promoted with eagerness to learn through the process of discovery rather than the child viewed as an empty vessel to be filled with facts. Encouraging children to think and attempt their ideas will support their creativity in dealing with challenges in the future. Clemson et al. (1994: 63) note 'the idea that mathematics is a subject for instruction rather than part of an education has its roots in the kind of mathematics curriculum offered nearly a century ago.' The Revised Code of 1862 contained statements about the attainment of standards, where children should learn a basic core of information and knowledge regarding subjects. In the early nineteenth century mathematics teaching was perceived as arithmetic. However, by the 1960s and the Plowden Report in 1967 there was an emphasis on children's exploration and understanding, through active learning and use of thinking skills.

Children's increasing knowledge of properties can be used to base problems concerning the area of learning. Activities can be planned to help children think creatively, solving problems and practical tasks based on length, weight, capacity and time.

Holistic development and shape, space and measures

There are various interpretations of the holistic development of children. An holistic approach could be viewed from a cross-curricular perspective to learning with shape, space and measures forming part of planning within other areas of learning. However, a broader perspective could view holistic development in terms of learning incorporating specific concepts and skills and personal, social and emotional aspects. The 'holistic ideology values the whole child and endeavours to understand each young child as an individual within the context of his or her family, community and culture. With this approach, professionals endeavour to be sensitive and responsive to all of a child's needs and aspects of development – that is physical, intellectual, social, emotional, cultural, moral and spiritual' (Woods, 2005: x). Petrie (2005: 294) suggests 'there is a growing awareness of the "whole" child or young person, rather than the child as the output of the formal curriculum.' This approach identifies that all experiences impact on a child's progress and influences how learning regarding shape, space and measures can be enhanced.

The EYFS framework identifies areas of development for the unique child, covering child development, inclusive practice, keeping safe and health and well-being.

In the early years areas of learning are intertwined and shape, space and measures can be successfully linked with other areas to enhance understanding and promote an holistic approach. Personal, social and emotional activities can include discussions of personal designs, encouraging self-esteem and value of own ideas, group work to share equipment and resources and collaborate between peers and adults concerning ideas.

Communication, Language and Literacy can be incorporated through written descriptions of designs and plans, links with activities, for example planned 3-D shaped presents given with letters.

Knowledge and Understanding of the World can be readily linked to shape, space and measures activities, through such activities as measurements of pathways in role-play stories, size of items used, shapes of made buildings in a map and space within it.

Elements of the area of learning can be represented as part of Creative Development, through such resources as painting or malleable materials. Physical Development can be incorporated, both indoors and outdoors, for example through games using shapes or differently shaped resources, or through manipulative skills when designing and drawing. Materials and cloth can be used for construction and encourage discussion and consideration of tessellating shapes, the properties of shapes, how size is relevant and an aware-ness of measurement gained. Play opportunities can be identified such as comparisons of the length of built towers, children when in lines or threaded beads.

Playdough, plasticine or clay can be measured, pulled, stretched and shaped to promote comparison and mathematical vocabulary such as longer/shorter while playing with the resources.

Weighing objects can be incorporated in activities, such as baking, the weight of different cars, small construction equipment or food items.

Case study

An ongoing resource to highlight awareness of shape, space and measures was created through the enhancement of the outdoor area in the setting. Children and parents and carers were asked to support the development of the facility to promote the area of learning. Features of their designs were incorporated into the plans for the outdoor area. The ideas included painted pictures on the ground which incorporated shapes, for example a boat and a snail; painted shapes on the ground used as part of games such as hopscotch, when practising road safety or throwing and catching, patterned foot prints when devising areas for cycle tracks or pathways.

Reflections for early career professional

- What resources can be used to support children's learning of shape, space and measures outdoors?

Reflections for leader/manager

- What provision is there for this aspect of learning in the outdoor space?
- How can shape, space and measures be promoted in your outdoor area?
- Can the provision provided be adapted for a wide range of uses, allowing for the children's creativity and imagination?

Photograph 3.1 Shapes in the outdoor area

This can form part of the general rationale for the provision for young children. Physical difficulties, for example with sight, could be a reason for a child's anxiety when distinguishing differently shaped objects or poor motor control could hamper the construction of shapes and spaces. These would need to be addressed within continuing practice.

Care needs to be taken when using resources, forming part of the overall attention needed when working with young children, for example the use of scissors for cutting shapes or making and using large 3-D constructions.

Awareness of different shapes and measures can be used by professionals working with the young children to promote a sense of self-knowledge and self-esteem. Their ideas can be celebrated to others in the setting and community to demonstrate their ideas are valued, for example their designs, calculations or pictures.

Teamwork of professionals and shape, space and measures

In order to successfully implement a holistic approach professionals work together for the benefit of children in their care. The EYFS puts the consideration of positive relationships into categories covering Respecting Each Other, Parents as Partners, Supporting Learning and key Person. Following this framework enables children to have a smooth transition both between providers and when they enter Key Stage 1. Children develop a growing awareness of mathematical concepts around them. Positive relationships with those around them help to expand children's excitement and enthusiasm for learning about mathematic knowledge and understanding in their world. Positive relationships can support inquisitive observations, explorations and investigations into the world through interacting in active play and learning while communicating and sharing ideas and experiences. Careful support of children's learning based on a child's desire to explore problems in the real-life contexts of their daily routines and play can build self-esteem and confidence in their own learning and the value of their ideas, thoughts and observations. Guidance of children's developing knowledge can be enhanced through questioning, sharing, consolidating and confirming their explorations. High expectations of children's abilities should be evident regardless of age, ability, gender or ethnicity. More able children should be sufficiently challenged to promote their learning. Children's understanding of properties of shape, space and measures can be enhanced through cooperative play with their peers and interactions with adults.

Case study

Children's interest in shape developed through observations of three fish which were brought into the setting. These were different shapes and caused much wonder and awe at their beauty while the fish swam in the large tank prepared for them. Observations were developed through reference to stories and non-fiction books about types of fish. Shapes of their bodies and fins were discussed and used as a basis for exploration with malleable materials to make made fish. These were painted, sorted, measured and shapes of fins noted. A large tank was constructed for their display using measurements and shapes in the process.

Photograph 3.2 Celebrating children's achievements in shape, space and measures

Partnerships can be strengthened through the development of this area of the curriculum. Planned links between activities and experiences at home can be incorporated into children's ideas and as part of the adult led-planned curriculum.

The Cockcroft Report (1982) cited in Clemson (1994: 22) stated that *'Parents can exercise, even unknowingly, a considerable influence on their children's attitudes to mathematics.'* The Plowden Report (1967) noted the impact parental interest on a child's development could have on the child's progress in learning. Published resources, such as IMPACT, promoted liaison between those working with young children, providing practical examples of activities which could be achieved between home and early years provision or school.

Activities to share with parents/carers could include ongoing tasks, such as sharing a book or song. Other activities could include linking tasks with topics that arise during the sessions, for example activities could be based on the theme. Travel and transport could include such activities as finding something that is a circle, using shapes to make a boat, finding shapes in a car or drawing a plan of a journey. Myself and Clothes could include using non-standard measures to chart height, making a patterned bracelet, ordering socks/shoes by size, collecting photos of babies and discussing how we have grown, drawing and comparing the size of feet in the family, considering ways of moving a certain distance, make a collage shape to put in a Shape Book in the setting or making a shape finger puppet. A project on Food could include collecting a spoon family, making a fairground ride, sorting fruit and vegetables by size, making a pasta clock, making a basket to carry fruit or baking biscuits, buns or a pizza. The theme of Families could include activities such as comparing the sizes of hands and feet, plotting the route home from the setting, finding shapes in the home or making shaped sandwiches. Living Things could include designing and planning a miniature garden, making an egg cup, designing and making a creature using boxes or cartons, using a pattern for a creature such as a snake or painting a symmetrical pattern on a picture of a butterfly. Toys could incorporate making a Toy Box, comparing the weight of toys, making a musical instrument or searching for squares.

Case study

A parent kindly donated a brightly coloured, attractive toybox for the setting. This led to activities based around the toybox, including the children making their own wooden boxes. One child, who had previously been successful at naming many shapes, sought to make his box. He drew a possible design and began. He carefully collected a circular shaped piece of wood and began to saw four square pieces of wood. Although he could state the properties of basic shapes with ease it was not until he placed the squares onto the circle that he really became aware of properties of circles and squares and tessellations. He had to rethink his original assumptions about his shapes then happily redesigned his project with overlaps from the circle forming the base.

Photograph 3.3 Activities displayed based on a toybox

Identified resources could be borrowed to share activities at home as well as in the setting.

According to Gifford (2005: 3) *'young children's performance varies greatly at school entry, with maturation and experience being particularly significant.'* Adults working in the setting can foster a desire to enrich children's opportunities to explore their expanding world in mathematical terms. They can draw on children's interests to develop meaningful contexts from their own ideas and thoughts, for their learning. Provision for a wide variety of practical experiences can extend children's mathematical learning and development. Support of the development of a precise mathematical vocabulary and its use in the correct contexts can be fostered by the adults working in the setting.

The key person who is the contact adult for the child has the opportunity to observe, interact and assess learning and development. Informal assessments occur when children undertake routine activities, such as awareness of place when hanging up a coat at the start of a session. Conversations with parents help to secure assessment judgements. Coordination of the recording of assessments between staff by the key person supports the smooth cycle of observation, assessment and planning. It supports the ability of adults in the setting to help children develop and share their ideas making them a positive contribution to activities in the provision. It is vital individual profiles are developed for each child for their care and identify any support they might need.

Good practice in shape, space and measures

Activities are most successful when they represent meaningful investigations and explorations for the children who are undertaking them. They are actively involved in their learning. Cross-curricular themes can include such tasks as keeping a record of the measurement of a growing plant. Reference needs to be made to the EYFS framework to provide a support for progression in children's learning through interactions and activities, rather than a haphazard approach where tasks occur in isolation. Children's prior learning is used to build on their next steps, for example activities based on toys can lead from an exploration of familiar toys, showing an interest in them and moving them in the space provided, to using toys in a construction activity, naming shapes needed to make a model and developing mathematical ideas to solve practical problems. Cross-curricular activities can support children's understanding of the properties as they work with problems posed.

Cross-curricular themes can include topics such as Ourselves, incorporating activities such as a comparison of sizes of family members, comparison of feet and hands, painted patterns using hands, feet, old shoes or boots, making patterned bracelets, measuring and making houses for teddy of plan of own home, construction of houses, for example for the three bears using large apparatus, discussion of bonded bricks, patterns of the bricks when building, measuring and making furniture using materials for construction or bought equipment, computer games based on Dressing Teddy or one based on Shapes, counting rhymes and songs, such as Build a House with Five Bricks, There were Ten in the Bed and sequencing time lines of events in the child's life. The theme of Toys can include activities such as using shapes to make toys, using shapes of fair rides, designing boxes for fruit or toys, sorting Autumn finds, designing shapes for musical toys, making puppets, using bubbles, balls and quoits, using shaped games outdoors, for example shaped beanbags, creating a Toyshop or making a box for a present. The topic Food can include designing and making 3-D food containers or sorting food and comparing for size and shape. The theme of Summer could incorporate activities such as making shaped sandwiches, biscuits, buns or pizzas for a picnic, using shapes to make pictures of growing things, making 3-D shaped vehicles for a journey in the sun, making pathways to plan journey for a holiday, sand play, such as sand pies or castles, rhymes and songs, such as five currant buns, ten green bottles, traditional stories such as Jack and the Beanstalk, a comparison of the sizes of fish, growing plants, baking, making shaped boats and water play.

Practical task

Ask children for their views on the enhancement of the outdoor space. Gain the support of parents/carers and the community in transforming the outdoor area of the setting, using expertise to develop the provision while seeking help to implement strategies suggested.

Leadership

Leaders of provision for young children consider such aspects as the enabling environment provided for children as individuals, the team whose ideas are valued and shared, appropriate resources for shape, space and measures, partnerships with parents and the wider community and celebration of achievements. The EYFS Principle into Practice card (DCSF, 2008) states *'Children must be supported in developing their understanding of Problem Solving, Reasoning and Numeracy in a broad range of contexts in which they can explore, enjoy, learn, practise and talk about their developing understanding. They must be provided with opportunities to practise these skills and to gain confidence and competence in their use.'*

Walshaw (2004: 124) suggests there is a need to evaluate those themes of learning that revolve around the idea of *'mental acquisition'*, rather that learning might be 'social' or 'culturally' constructed by an engagement or discussion with others. This develops in part from Vygotsky's theory of social interactions building understanding. Ernest has a social constructivist view of mathematics. Ernest (1991, cited, ibid: 124) contends that mathematics is not viewed as a fixed entity *'but as a set of diverse multi-centred socially situated practices across time, space and institutional locations, making use of different textual forms to embody mathematical knowledge'*. If this is the case leaders of providers are required to respond to and implement new initiatives and changes. Changing structures in *societies 'place complex and sometimes conflicting demands on us in ways we are barely able to understand or predict'* (Walshaw, 2004: 2). She notes *'Increasingly we are becoming aware of the complex construction of our work within the discipline emerging from, among other things, new forms of inclusive political tendencies, changing vocational needs and advances in information and communication systems.'* However, the increasingly new perspectives *'do not map easily onto traditional understandings about the known and the knower'* (Walshaw, 2004: 3).

Mathematical understanding can be incorporated into the enabling environment to ensure children have access to a range of learning styles and exciting possibilities to explore ideas and concepts. This can be achieved through adult-led and children's independent activities and the leader and the team can plan the enabling environment to ensure such facilities are available for the children in their care. This can include providing appropriate resources, incorporating both made equipment and materials for children to design and make their own specifications. They can form part of the daily routines of the setting. Awareness of aspects of the area can be explored both indoors and outdoors. The natural environment can be used to promote the understanding of mathematical vocabulary and concepts. Buildings, trees, flowers etc. can be used as a focus for enquiry. Space within the provision can be organized to promote a variety of exploration regarding the area of learning, for example large special areas to manage construction work, graphic areas to support the formulation of designs, readily labelled and resources organized to facilitate ease of access, the whole area of the setting indoors, outdoors or a covered area outdoors.

Opportunities should be given for children to record their findings in their play. A range of coloured paper or card including flip charts, clip boards and white boards with various mark making equipment should be readily available to enable children to practise their emergent marks as part of their play activities. Books incorporating mathematical concepts, both fiction and non-fiction, should be displayed as a source of reference for the children to use. In autumn a setting based work on leaves, sorting, counting, using non-standard measures and comparing differently shaped leaves to heighten awareness of key mathematical points. Harvest fruit was estimated and counted. Children used clip boards to record the shapes observed and the numbers counted.

Interactive displays focusing on the area of learning can enhance understanding, for example matching shapes, counting children on a bus or car ride or making patterns. Children can take responsibility for changing the achievements on display as their growing knowledge of certain aspects develop and progress. These interactions support the scaffolding of children's understanding of elements of shape, space and measures. Number lines can incorporate written and mathematical numbers, pictures to aid correspondence and 3-D apparatus to provide kinaesthetic support.

The organization of the day and timings can facilitate continuation and consolidation of ideas to support children's progress in their learning, for example key timings can be observed with the children, such as starting a session at 9 a.m. or eating lunch at noon. Shapes can be observed on an ongoing basis, for example sandwich shapes, shapes and sizes of the equipment or resources such as drinking cups or plates.

Observation, assessment and planning

There are a wide variety of assessments available to identify where a child is in the Learning, Development and Care area of the framework.

The Williams Report (2008: 41) notes the importance of considering individual scale points rather than simply perusing the total scores. Groupings of children can support an individual child's progress, with differing teams promoting social interaction and enhanced thinking. These can be planned into the routine of the day. Time can also be spent throughout the day or in the plenary highlighting achievements.

The learning environment

The enabling environment should be carefully thought out to provide the best possible facilities for the children who attend. A welcoming, safe and stimulating environment will strengthen the development and learning while providing a positive, happy area where children and adults will want to be. Provision for shape, space and measures will be addressed both as an area of learning in its own right and as part of the broad spectrum of learning about the world within the other areas of learning and development. In order to achieve this the area could be considered to ensure aspects are being covered and children are aware of it. The bright, colourful environment can include displays in places such as the entrance, where attractive examples of children's work for the parents/carers and children to discuss together can be displayed, such as children's own self-portraits in shaped frames or 2-D shaped collage pictures incorporating questions about their work, for example how many squares are in the pictures? A specific table or area to focus attention on areas such as pattern, shape and measures can be incorporated in the enabling environment of the setting. Cross-curricular learning opportunities can develop children's interests while drawing out aspects of shape, space and measures, for example shaped utensils to match at a table/cooking area.

Aspects of the problem solving, reasoning and numeracy area of learning and development form a major part of the early years framework. Children sort, match and count objects; develop mathematical language; learn about the number system, for example through handling money, singing and reciting number songs and rhymes; extending their spatial awareness through movement and handling objects; develop ideas of sequence, pattern and order.

All mathematical experiences are presented many times in a wide variety of contexts and in numerous different ways. These experiences gradually increase in length, level of difficulty, complexity of language and type of instructions given, for example younger children explore shapes and construct. Older children will consider pattern, how shapes can interlock, be aware of the properties and names of shapes.

Most equipment/apparatus is used at a variety of different levels and it will provide for a range of possible learning outcomes. Children's activities will incorporate an increasing amount of their internalizing and visualizing the properties to support their tasks. Small group table top games can be available alongside larger apparatus and used as a regular ongoing resource. Within the early years setting a specific area for problem solving, reasoning and measures can be combined with planning for the area of learning throughout the framework. Resources for the children should be at an appropriate height for ease of access and to enable the child to put them away tidily after their play. Labelling of boxed equipment with pictures particularly for the youngest children, support their understanding of vocabulary and meaning of print.

Areas should be organized to provide space for children to develop large constructions or quietly work on a mark making design. Considered space for groupings of children can support solitary thinking, small group interactions or large group discussions.

The outdoor space should be fully utilized to form part of the learning environment for the child. Activities begun indoors can be developed outdoors, while the outdoor environment can promote new challenges for the child, such as games using painted shapes on the playground or finding shapes in the natural world.

Suggested resources include home/school resources to share with parents/carers. The items are listed in groups but can be used in other parts of the area of learning.

Reflections for early career professionals

- Can activities be planned to incorporate consolidation of learning, building on children's prior knowledge?

Reflections for leader /manager

- Consider whether interactive activities for children have been used to the full in your provision, for example matching shapes stored in different areas, using sand or water equipment to discuss shape and size when storing it for children's independent use.
- Consider how children access the resources and tidy away. Are learning opportunities used during these activities?

Shape and Space Resources

- 3-D shapes from the natural world to foster children's interests for example, conkers, acorns, differently shaped leaves
- 3-D shapes – boxes, cartons, etc.
- 3-D equipment for example, shaped beanbags, balls, tunnels
- 3-D games for example, postbox for shapes
- Sets of equipment 3-D and 2-D shapes for example, polydron, clixi, logiblocks, patterns, blocks
- Multilink cubes
- Hoops, baskets etc. for sorting
- Plastic shapes, eggmen
- Plastic mirrors
- Puzzles
- Jigsaws these could be sorted for difficulty to ensure a range of jigsaws are available for children
- Large construction equipment
- Small construction equipment
- Materials to make own 3-D shapes
- Dens, climbing apparatus, pathways
- Compasses
- Malleable materials and equipment for example, pastry cutters
- Non-fiction and fiction books based on shape and space
- Mark making materials for example, pencils, paints, large and small paper
- Examples of pattern for example, on cards, material
- Own made patterns for example, repeated patterns, patterns with shapes
- Equipment for sorting and matching
- Own made equipment to sort/match
- Pattern apparatus or games
- Printing with one side of a 3-D shape
- Play in sand and water

Measures resources

- Fiction and non-fiction books based on measures for example, containing comparison of size; heavy, light
- Collections of natural, made and children's own items for comparison
- Rulers, tape measures
- Programmable toys for example, Roamer, Beebots
- String, mark making materials
- Non-standard measures for example of children
- Utensils for cooking for example, scales, various sizes of pans
- Recipe cards, recipe books, shopping lists, children's own recipe books
- Balances and weights

- Collection of materials to sort/compare for weight
- Plasticine and playdough
- Collection of non-fiction and fiction books about time
- Materials to record weather
- Daily weather chart
- A working analogue clock to discuss as part of routine with children
- Plastic and cardboard clock faces
- Clock stamps
- Timing games, elating time to own experiences for example, time for a story, home time, days of the week, night/day, yesterday, today, tomorrow
- Tockers
- Stopwatch
- Teaching clock
- Messages from adults for example, 'There are five more minutes before tidying away.'

Water activities incorporate:

- Interaction with peers and adults
- Imaginative play
- Discovery
- Co-operation and sharing equipment
- Listening to instructions from each other and adults
- Perseverance with a self-chosen or set task
- Remembers past experiences and learning
- Compares wet and dry
- Compares volume
- Explores fluidity for example, finds its own level, flows downhill
- Sorts for capacity
- Shows one-to-one correspondence
- Develops fine motor skills, such as pouring, filling, emptying, splashing, washing, wiping, bathing, painting with colour

Activities with sand include

- Talk to peers and adults
- Imaginative play
- Discussion of discoveries
- Learns new vocabulary and uses it with understanding
- Shares tasks, tools and sand
- Listens and responds to others
- Perseveres with a certain task
- Remembers past experiences and discoveries
- Compares wet and dry sand

- Compares textures
- Compares weights and volume
- Uses correct tools for a particular task
- Develops fine motor skills such as filling, emptying, dividing, patting, sieving, digging, raking, shovelling, tunnelling, pushing/pulling
- Keeps resources tidy and safe, using dustpan and brush

Case study

Activities based on shapes led to means for displaying children's ideas. These were made into a book and stored in the book corner, to enable children to browse through the pictures and designs at their leisure. They were also displayed to provide an interactive focal point for discussion about properties of shapes. Later in the year the development of children's ideas about the use of shapes led to collage work based on the shape pictures and patterns which were used as presents, such as incorporated into calendars.

Photograph 3.4 Collage shapes used to sew pictures

Shapes

Haylock (1995: 179) states *'Classification is an important intellectual process which helps to make sense of our experiences.'*

Polygons

Polygons are closed plane shapes with straight sides. Regular polygons have all their sides and all their angles equal.

Common polygons include:

Triangle – three sides
Quadrilateral – four sides
Pentagon – five sides
Hexagon – six sides
Heptagon – seven sides
Octagon – eight sides

Triangles are named to describe their sides.

Equilateral triangle – All three sides equal, therefore three angles equal
Isosceles triangle – Two sides equal therefore two angles equal
Scalene triangle – Sides all different lengths, therefore all angles different

Quadrilaterals include:

Parallelogram – Opposite sides equal and parallel, opposite angles equal
Rhombus – Opposite sides equal and parallel, opposite sides equal, two lines of symmetry. Parallelogram with adjacent sides equal
Rectangle – Opposite sides equal and parallel, opposite angles equal Parallelogram with four right angles
Square – Opposite sides equal and parallel, four lines of symmetry Parallelogram with four right angles and adjacent sides equal
Oblong – Opposite sides equal and parallel, opposite angles equal, two lines of symmetry Rectangle with adjacent sides of different length
Trapezium – One pair of opposite sides parallel
Kite – Two pairs of adjacent sides equal

The wider context

The indoors and outdoors provision in the early years settings provides a foundation for the children's learning. This can be enhanced and developed through the broader input from the wider context. Partnerships with parents can offer a shared approach to the development of the children. This can be extended to the wider community through visits in the locality, such as the park or shops, following the settings health and safety policies. A visit to a shop can promote awareness of space while planning the route taken and observing places of interest on the journey, mathematical vocabulary used in liaison and discussions with staff and children to decide what the groups needed and the shopping required, mark making for the shopping lists and the route, spatial awareness of the layout of the shop, shapes of the bought items and sorting and counting of items.

A visit to the park can foster making maps of the park, discussion of the route taken from the setting to the park, consideration of shapes in the environment and measurement of distances in the park.

These experiences can stimulate interest in the setting and motivate children to design their own shop or park, measuring resources to achieve this and finding out how shapes will interlock to provide appropriate structures. Role play of shops can incorporate sorting items by shape, marking making for lists of shopping, matching items and interactions with others for the cooperation of the play. Inclusion issues can readily be addressed, through careful planning for individuals within the setting. A multicultural environment can be forged through such strategies as multilingual signs and posters.

Children's interests can be expanded through visitors to the setting, for example a music session taken by a visiting musician, following appropriate policies, can lead to measurements while making own instruments or sorting instruments by shape.

Reflections for early career professionals

- Can children's understanding of shape, space and measures be planned for as a link with home/setting practice, for example drawing on children's knowledge of visits to the shops?

Reflections for leader/manager

- Reflect on the learning environment. Is the environment suitably resourced for a range of learning and teaching styles?
- Are the staff working in the enabling environment supported to share opportunities when they arise to promote this area of the curriculum?
- Is the learning environment appropriate for children to develop their own ideas and understanding of shape, space and measures?
- Are display opportunities being utilized to celebrate children's achievements?

References

Clemson, D. and Clemson, W. (1994), *Mathematics in the Early Years*. London: Routledge.

DCSF (2008), *The Early Years Foundation Stage; Setting the Standard for Learning, Development and Care for Children aged Birth to Five; Practice Guidance* London: DCSF

Gifford, S (2005), *Young Children's Difficulties in Learning Mathematics*. Roehampton, University of Surrey: Qualifications and Curriculum Authority

Haylock, D. (1995), *Mathematics Explained*. London: Paul Chapman Publishing Ltd.

Haylock, D. Cockburn, A. (1989), *Understanding Early Years Mathematics*. London: Paul Chapman Publishing Ltd.

Hopkins, C., Gifford, S. and Pepperell, S. (1999), *Mathematics in the Primary School: A Sense of Progression*. London: David Fulton Publishers

Nutbrown, C. and Page, J. (2008), *Working with Babies and Children*. London: Sage

Petrie, P (2005), Extending Pedagogy *Journal of Education for Teaching*, 31, (4) London: Routledge.

Pound, L. (2003), *Supporting Mathematical Development in the Early Years*. Buckingham: Open University Press

Walshaw, M. (ed.) (2004), *Mathematics Education within the Postmodern*. Connecticut: Information Age Publishing.

Williams, P. (2008), *Independent Review of Mathematical Teaching in Early Years Settings and Primary Schools*. Nottingham: DCSF

Woods, T. (2005), *Beginning Postmodernity*. Manchester: Manchester University Press

Conclusion

The series editors and authors hope that you find this book of interest and use to you in your professional work. If you would like to read more about the subject area, we recommend the following reading and websites to you.

Further reading

Askew, M., Bibby, T. and Brown, M. (2001), *Raising Attainment in Primary Number Sense: From Counting to Strategy*. London: BEAM Education Research Papers

Drews, D. and Hansen, A. (2007), *Using Resources to Support Mathematical Thinking: Primary and Early Years*. Exeter: Learning Matters

Skinner, C. (2005), *Maths Outdoors*. London: BEAM

Skinner, A. (2008), *Maths Inside and Out*. London: BEAM

Useful websites

BEAM – Be a Mathematician: Resources, articles, courses
   www.beam.co.uk
National Centre for Excellence in the Teaching of Mathematics
   www.ncetm.org.uk
Nrich – maths investigations, interactive games, articles, advice, CPD
   http://nrich.maths.org
Teachers tv – videos and resources
   www.teachers.tv

If you would like to read more about other key areas of the Early Years Foundation Stage, please see the following:

Callander, N and Nahmad-Williams, N. (2010), *Communication, Language and Literacy*, London: Continuum

Compton, A., Johnston, J., Nahmad-Williams, L and Taylor, K. (2010), *Creative Development*. London: Continuum

Cooper, L., Johnston, J., Rotchell, E. and Woolley, R. (2010), *Knowledge and Understanding of the World*, London: Continuum

Broadhead, P., Johnston, J., Tobbell, C. and Woolley, R. (2010), *Personal, Social and Emotional Development*. London: Continuum

Cooper, L. and Doherty, J. (2010), *Physical Development*. London: Continuum

Index